866-840-4334
http://www.timebeing.com

Ben Milder
From Adolescence to Senescence: A Life in Light Verse
The Good Book Also Says . . . : Numerous Humorous Poems Inspired by the New Testament
The Good Book Says . . . : Light Verse to Illuminate the Old Testament
Love Is Funny, Love Is Sad
What's So Funny About the Golden Years
The Zoo You Never Gnu: A Mad Menagerie of Bizarre Beasts and Birds

Charles Muñoz
Fragments of a Myth: Modern Poems on Ancient Themes

Micheal O'Siadhail
The Gossamer Wall: Poems in Witness to the Holocaust

Joseph Stanton
A Field Guide to the Wildlife of Suburban O'ahu
Imaginary Museum: Poems on Art

Susan Terris
Contrariwise

866-840-4334
http://www.timebeing.com

David Herrle
Abyssinia, Jill Rush

William Heyen
Erika: Poems of the Holocaust
Falling from Heaven: Holocaust Poems of a Jew and a Gentile *(Brodsky and Heyen)*
The Host: Selected Poems, 1965–1990
Pterodactyl Rose: Poems of Ecology
Ribbons: The Gulf War — A Poem

Ted Hirschfield
German Requiem: Poems of the War and the Atonement of a Third Reich Child

Virginia V. James Hlavsa
Waking October Leaves: Reanimations by a Small-Town Girl

Rodger Kamenetz
The Missing Jew: New and Selected Poems
Stuck: Poems Midlife

Norbert Krapf
Blue-Eyed Grass: Poems of Germany
Looking for God's Country
Somewhere in Southern Indiana: Poems of Midwestern Origins

Adrian C. Louis
Blood Thirsty Savages

Leo Luke Marcello
Nothing Grows in One Place Forever: Poems of a Sicilian American

Gardner McFall
The Pilot's Daughter
Russian Tortoise

Joseph Meredith
Hunter's Moon: Poems from Boyhood to Manhood
Inclinations of the Heart

866-840-4334
http://www.timebeing.com

Louis Daniel Brodsky (continued)
Three Early Books of Poems by Louis Daniel Brodsky, 1967–1969: *The Easy Philosopher*, *"A Hard Coming of It" and Other Poems*, and *The Foul Rag-and-Bone Shop*
Toward the Torah, Soaring: Poems of the Renascence of Faith
A Transcendental Almanac: Poems of Nature
Voice Within the Void: Poems of *Homo supinus*
With One Foot in the Butterfly Farm *(short fictions)*
The World Waiting to Be: Poems About the Creative Process
Yellow Bricks *(short fictions)*
You Can't Go Back, Exactly

Harry James Cargas (editor)
Telling the Tale: A Tribute to Elie Wiesel on the Occasion of His 65th Birthday — Essays, Reflections, and Poems

Judith Chalmer
Out of History's Junk Jar: Poems of a Mixed Inheritance

Gerald Early
How the War in the Streets Is Won: Poems on the Quest of Love and Faith

Gary Fincke
Blood Ties: Working-Class Poems

Charles Adès Fishman
Blood to Remember: American Poets on the Holocaust *(editor)*
Chopin's Piano

CB Follett
Hold and Release

Albert Goldbarth
A Lineage of Ragpickers, Songpluckers, Elegiasts & Jewelers: Selected Poems of Jewish Family Life, 1973–1995

Robert Hamblin
Crossroads: Poems of a Mississippi Childhood
From the Ground Up: Poems of One Southerner's Passage to Adulthood
Keeping Score: Sports Poems for Every Season

Other Poetry and Short Fictions Available from Time Being Books

Yakov Azriel
Beads for the Messiah's Bride: Poems on Leviticus
In the Shadow of a Burning Bush: Poems on Exodus
Threads from a Coat of Many Colors: Poems on Genesis

Edward Boccia
No Matter How Good the Light Is: Poems by a Painter

Louis Daniel Brodsky
At Water's Edge: Poems of Lake Nebagamon, Volume One
By Leaps and Bounds: Volume Two of *The Seasons of Youth*
The Capital Café: Poems of Redneck, U.S.A.
Catchin' the Drift o' the Draft *(short fictions)*
Combing Florida's Shores: Poems of Two Lifetimes
The Complete Poems of Louis Daniel Brodsky: Volumes One–Four
Dine-Rite: Breakfast Poems
Disappearing in Mississippi Latitudes: Volume Two of *A Mississippi Trilogy*
The Eleventh Lost Tribe: Poems of the Holocaust
Falling from Heaven: Holocaust Poems of a Jew and a Gentile *(Brodsky and Heyen)*
Forever, for Now: Poems for a Later Love
Four and Twenty Blackbirds Soaring
Gestapo Crows: Holocaust Poems
Getting to Unknow the Neighbors *(short fictions)*
A Gleam in the Eye: Volume One of *The Seasons of Youth*
Leaky Tubs *(short fictions)*
Mississippi Vistas: Volume One of *A Mississippi Trilogy*
Mistress Mississippi: Volume Three of *A Mississippi Trilogy*
Nuts to You! *(short fictions)*
Once upon a Small-Town Time: Poems of America's Heartland
Paper-Whites for Lady Jane: Poems of a Midlife Love Affair
Peddler on the Road: Days in the Life of Willy Sypher
Pigskinizations *(short fictions)*
Rabbi Auschwitz: Poems of the Shoah
Rated Xmas *(short fictions)*
Seizing the Sun and Moon: Volume Three of *The Seasons of Youth*
Shadow War: A Poetic Chronicle of September 11 and Beyond, Volumes One–Five
Showdown with a Cactus: Poems Chronicling the Prickly Struggle
  Between the Forces of Dubya-ness and Enlightenment, 2003–2006
Still Wandering in the Wilderness: Poems of the Jewish Diaspora
This Here's a Merica *(short fictions)*
The Thorough Earth

Biographical Note

Louis Daniel Brodsky was born in St. Louis, Missouri, in 1941, where he attended St. Louis Country Day School. After earning a B.A., magna cum laude, at Yale University in 1963, he received an M.A. in English from Washington University in 1967 and an M.A. in Creative Writing from San Francisco State University the following year.

From 1968 to 1987, while continuing to write poetry, he assisted in managing a 350-person men's-clothing factory in Farmington, Missouri, and started one of the Midwest's first factory-outlet apparel chains. From 1980 to 1991, he taught English and creative writing, part-time, at Mineral Area College, in nearby Flat River. Since 1987, he has lived in St. Louis and devoted himself to composing poems and short fictions. He has a daughter and a son.

Brodsky is the author of seventy volumes of poetry (five of which have been published in French by Éditions Gallimard) and twenty-four volumes of prose, including nine books of scholarship on William Faulkner and nine books of short fictions. His poems and essays have appeared in *Harper's*, *Faulkner Journal*, *Southern Review*, *Texas Quarterly*, *National Forum*, *American Scholar*, *Studies in Bibliography*, *Kansas Quarterly*, *Forum*, *Cimarron Review*, and *Literary Review*, as well as in *Ariel*, *Acumen*, *Orbis*, *New Welsh Review*, *Dalhousie Review*, and other journals. His work has also been printed in five editions of the *Anthology of Magazine Verse and Yearbook of American Poetry*.

In 2004, Brodsky's *You Can't Go Back, Exactly* won the award for best book of poetry, presented by the Center for Great Lakes Culture, at Michigan State University.

Poem Suites

The chapters in this volume reflect the structure of poetry suites Louis Daniel Brodsky wrote during visits to Lake Nebagamon, Wisconsin. The dates of composition for these suites are as follows:

May Gusts and Silences (5/17–5/21/09)
Independence Days (6/26–7/8/09)
The Stars, the Clouds, and the Lake (8/14–8/23/09)
Sunrises and Sunsets (9/18–9/27/09)
Christmastide in the Village (12/23/09–1/2/10)

Epilogue

A Lake

Everyone should have a lake in the valley of his soul,
A body of water and a shore to contain it,
Give it a shape that imagination can embrace,

A refuge to which world-weary journeyers can retreat,
To restore the forgotten pleasures of the heart:
Tranquillity, solitude, solemnity, serenity, calm,

The sense of peace that draws its seekers inward,
Beckoning them to peer into the lake's depths,
Connect with its intellect, the essence of its prescience,

The life-force that gives its molecules mellifluous integrity,
Heals those who repair to its shores, to bathe,
Redeems them of their ennui, makes them whole, sacred.

XXIV. The End of the Dock

The sun is eight minutes late to its 7:50 ascension.
This delay isn't its fault but mine — vision's limitation,
For the forest bordering Lake Nebagamon,
Blocking, from my sight, its climb out of night,
Its second rising of the new year.

And what difference might it possibly make to me, anyway,
Since, on this mildly hazy a.m.
(My last full day here,
Before I call this trip, with melancholy, a memory),
It'll labor, in vain, to warm this shivering land appreciably?

It's minus 19.1 degrees, just beyond my windowpanes.
All I can see is stark-white silence's bare reality,
Neither frightening nor inviting, so much as just there,
A force to contend with, if I dare venture out,
Intend to test my mettle, against its intractable presence.

At this frigid, fragile, frozen, freighted moment,
Only three black crows are stirring,
Flying back and forth, between the lake's surface
And the giant pine in my cabin's side lot —
An activity not apt to fatten their famished bodies.

Curious, I get up from the kitchen table,
To check the thermometer, see if the sun's made a difference.
Now, at nine o'clock, it registers minus 12.8.
At this rate, by late April, when the ice should be melted,
Or at least as mid-May green awakens around the lake,

I'll be able to walk out on my dock again
(Which, sadly, is dismantled, on the shore below,
Its two wheel-mounted sections mired in snow),
And sit at its end, listening, daydreaming, meditating
To waves rippling, whispering, singing water-spirit songs.

XXIII. Off Lorber Point

Knowing the sun will set one minute before 4:30,
I tighten my snowshoes' bindings, grasp my ski pole,
And enter the woods, by Camp Nebagamon's back gate,

Take to the road, pass the Lumberjack Village cabins,
Veer left at the Herb Hollinger Museum,
And head through the pine forest, toward Lorber Point,

Trudging over knee-deep snow,
In the face of the rapidly descending, blazing fireball.
Drawing near, I begin tearing fiercely.

It's the wind, this ferocious New Year's Day wind,
Whipping my eyes, punishing them unremittingly,
Causing them to distort the trees into blurry surrealities.

In desperation, I turn away from the blasting air,
Follow Spitting Spring Trail maybe a hundred yards,
Hoping to see day dissolve into mellow twilight pastels.

Then, unexpectedly, my snowshoes become divining rods,
Guiding me off the narrow, labyrinthine path,
Through bare, brittle, brown underbrush, down to the shore.

What, minutes ago, was a half-degree-above-zero chill
Is, now, out on the lake's frozen, snow-gessoed surface,
A blistering fifteen to twenty below.

Although snowshoeing is far less effort to sustain, out here,
The gusts, penetrating my gloves, boots, neck gaiter,
Striking at my fingers, toes, lips, nose, eyes, are bitterly painful.

Nonetheless, I stop, gaze just above Minnesuing Creek,
As the flaming orb disappears, with a silent flourish,
Its roses, oranges, purples, mauves leaching across the sky.

For endless seconds, my flesh, bones, senses aren't mine;
They're impervious to the murderous cold. My blood runs hot,
As though the last of day's rays are racing through my veins.

Hearing the lake moaning deep within the ice's soul,
As if it were empathizing with my puny humanity,
I know, in these mortal moments, what it's like to be eternal.

XXII. Midnight

Quietude, isolation, serenity, and grass-roots happiness
Are the melodious leitmotifs I play over and over,
This biting Thursday night — New Year's Eve.

The cabin keeps me wombed in warmth.
The lake, slowly flowing beneath silence's ice,
Is the water that surrounds my gestating imagination.

I join myself late, at my book-cluttered kitchen table.
We share a lettuce-tomato-crouton salad, wine,
Leftover pasta with vegetables, savor raspberries, blueberries,

Before I dress, in my coat of many necessary layers,
Adjust boots, gloves, neck gaiter, cap, hood, and parka,
Then step out, into the clear, windless, zero-degree midnight air,

Just in time to see the five-minute fireworks display
(Sponsored by the village's two bars and Lawn Beach Inn)
Flying up, from the municipal beach, at the foot of Lake Avenue,

Illuminating the dark auditorium, festive restaurant next door,
Its echoing reports and dazzling flashes of phosphorescence
Announcing the momentous advent of 2010.

Even after the too-brief tumult recedes into the lingering past,
I look up, peering through my breath's diaphanous smoke,
Remain focused on the myriad stars, the lunar wafer,

And realize that the sky is attending its own celebration,
Marking one more manifestation of its glorious being,
Neither ignoring me nor imploring me to record its ubiquity.

I stay longer than my fingers and toes tell me I should,
Reluctant to walk back to my cabin
Without inviting the full moon to come sleep with me.

XXI. Locus

For the ten days I've been here,
The compact car I rented at the airport
Has remained cold and dark, parked by the front door.

The watch I wore, on my left wrist,
During my flight from St. Louis to Duluth, via Minneapolis,
Has hibernated on the kitchen table.

The newspaper I bought at home, brought with me,
Intending to catch up on national and world events,
Has wilted, atop a carton of bottled water.

Not once have I used my cell phone.
If anyone's called, I wouldn't know; it's been turned off.
Silence is very close to being golden.

In this timeless place, where my legs are my transportation
And I have no need to read about the state of mankind
Or stay in touch with people and their grandiosities,

I've achieved, if not the quintessence of mind peace,
At least the essence of independence and self-reliance
Required to find my locus in nature's soul.

XX. Last Day of the Year

It's one thing to wish for, ask for, pray for snow
On Christmas Eve
And receive it as a blessing from heaven
Or surrogate infiniteness
In which one may invest spirituality,

But it's altogether another thing
To wish for, ask for, pray for snow,
A continuous dusting, anyway, if not a blizzard,
On New Year's Eve
And get a second benediction of divine will.

Ah, but here I am, in the North Woods,
This last day of 2009,
Circumscribed by a shimmering snowy halo,
Glowing like a full moon,
Welcoming the coming of wondrous times.

XIX. Other Beauty

I've been a frequent resident of this Wisconsin enclave,
But never in the winter,
And I'm out of sync with every element enveloping me.

I'll never get used to such pervasive, lingering whiteness.
My eyes sense it strange, implausible, surreal
That the lake and sky are mirror images of each other.

More disorienting, ten days into my sojourn,
I've caught barely a blur of a furry creature or bird,
Mostly just tracks in the snow, flakes flying in the sky.

I'm thrown by being encumbered with cold-weather clothing,
When I wend through the demanding woods,
And, otherwise, finding myself confined to this cabin.

Not that I really mind this much solitude, isolation;
I favor the company of books, music, meditation,
Over small conversation with too-large egos.

Indeed, up here, I'm beginning to see, feel, learn
That winter's exaggerations, idiosyncrasies, inconveniences
Are what make its severe beauty visible to me.

XVIII. Snowshoeing, Late Afternoon

So much for the brisk-clip walks
Of this past year's visits to Lake Nebagamon's village.
Now, of necessity, my speed has measurably tapered
To a tortoise's plodding, the flowing of glaciers.
It's slow as she goes; the steadier the better. I should know.

This is my fifth hike into the camp and its woodlands,
And each occasion has been a lifelong education.
The gray, snowy day doesn't penetrate my winter armor,
Even as I enter deeper into the quiet beckoning,
Lean forward, into every sinking, crunching step I take,

Passing landlocked boats, docks, Lumberjack cabins,
Heading beyond the shrine, ball field, to the council ring,
Where I stop to rest, pay homage to the totem pole,
Focus on its nine symbolic images,
A spread-winged eagle at the top, "1936" at the bottom.

Only my mind's eye can see the hidden firepit's design.
The stark wooden benches
Are occupied by twenty inches of accumulated drifts —
Row upon row of campers and staff
Gathered for a summer Sunday night's secular sacraments.

Soon, I'm by the tennis courts, then the Swamper cabins,
Which, now that their green roofs are white
(Matching the exact shade of their antique clapboard siding),
Blend into the purlieus, through which I slip undetected,
Even by my own keen vision.

After an hour and a half, from beginning to finish,
Unfatigued, indeed exhilarated *and* relaxed,
I unstrap the bindings of my intricately webbed snowshoes
And walk in my boots (no less slowly, for the ice underfoot),
Marveling at having exited, into dusk, so revitalized.

XVII. Forecast

This afternoon might be the last time,
For the next three days or so,
That I'll be able to go snowshoeing in the boys' camp,
For a biting, fiercely blowing wind being forecast,
One so vicious,
It can make you feel as if the flesh on your face
Were being peeled away, a layer at a time,
With a blunt scalpel.

I need to take advantage, without hesitation,
Of whatever random chances
Nature throws my way, advances me.
I think that, now, right this 15.7-degree hour,
I'd better get myself out of this heated cabin,
Revel in one more ecstatic go at the cold,
In the snow-enfolded, pine-silent woods,
Before my eager heartbeat freezes.

XVI. Two Faces of the Lake

Yesterday, under a penetrating sun,
The snow-coated lake was a diamond,
Its millions of flake-facets
Casting lustrous glints
That set the bordering forests afire,
Turning each tree into a solar flare
That never melted the snow to opaque slush.

Today, under a drab, mottled-gray sky
Intermittently spitting confetti,
The lake ice is a white scab
Stretching, to its undulating shoreline,
Over dormant water
Praying it won't take until late April
For the groaning wound to heal.

XV. Holiday Travels

This persistently chilled Christmastide,
While spending my holidays here in Lake Nebagamon,
I've visited Depression-era Bedford Falls,
Met George Bailey and his childhood-sweetheart wife, Mary,
In the postwar frames of *It's a Wonderful Life*.

Now, two nights before New Year's Eve,
I'm traveling to Moscow, during the people's purge of the czar,
Being transported, in a cattle car, to Yuriatin, in the Urals,
And sleighing to Varykino, where I'll stay in an icebound dacha,
With Yuri and Lara, through the lens-pen of *Dr. Zhivago*.

The threads interlacing these three snowy locations,
Spanning a century, have everything to do with me,
My poetic weaver's capacity
To stitch artistic time into compatible magical fabrics
That my spirit can wear when it's unspeakably cold.

For years, I've hoped to juxtapose these two movies,
Show them on my North Woods screen, in winter,
Let them ferry my imagination to the edges of despair,
Remind me just how fleeting our passions can be,
For suffering the cruelties inflicted by our too-human doings,

How hopeless the days doled out to our destinies can be,
When fate becomes such an indifferent, prodigal apostate,
How conflicted our relationships with ourselves can be,
And how, when personal turmoil storms our dreams,
Love can warm our chilled hearts, our shivering souls.

XIV. Measuring Sunrises

As it was, yesterday, and will be, for the next ten a.m.'s,
Sunrise is due at precisely 7:50,
And with passing weeks, it will burst earlier and earlier,

Until, at the far end of March, when I'm here again,
Dawn will have found a new waking hour,
In the late six o'clocks.

This morning, brewing coffee, I linger in the dark,
Listening to the cabin's conspicuous sounds,
Knowing that, though distracting, they sustain me.

The kitchen's refrigerator motor, cycling erratically,
Doesn't mask the crotchety complaints of the furnace,
Which curses me, for my insisting it put in overtime,

As does the water heater,
And it tells me so, in outspoken, all-too-certain terms,
With its frigid pipes' clanking, knocking, screeching

Keeping sleep out of easy reach.
And yet, I'm happier here, nestled in, beside the lake,
Than I've been in a score of disconsolate years.

It all hinges on measuring time by my own calibrations,
Not society's expectations, which regulate each tocktick
By the dollar signs piling up, minute to minute.

Now, with not quite an hour before sunrise becomes official,
The horizon just above the saw-toothed tops
Of pines, spruces, leafless maples, ashes, and birches

Is glimmering with an orange-and-rose glow,
Just below a near-cloudless layer of cerulean hues
That promise to give the emerging sun complete freedom.

Curious, how, from my stifled cityscape locations,
I always assume that day and night have a sharp demarcation,
That, as in Genesis, there's "dark" and there's "light."

How illuminating it is, for me, to realize, come to believe,
That futures arrive not as black-or-white abstractions,
Rather in gradations, gradually.

Now, it's almost nine.
I've dined on two bowls of robust vegetable soup, Italian bread,
Toasted, with red wine, the ice, snow, ten-above-zero cold,

And it's time for me to say good night, go to bed,
Filled with praises for another day in which all that mattered
Was satisfying my appetite for delicious simplicity.

XIII. Vegetable-Soup Afternoon

On a sunny Monday afternoon as harsh as this one,
I can hardly think of any activity more comforting
Than preparing an eight-quart pot of vegetable soup, for supper.

Days ago, I supplied my accommodating cabin's larder
With all the ingredients requisite for my lengthy stay.
But if forgetting tells me so, I can always walk uptown, to Ole's;

After all, it takes only six minutes to get there,
Five minutes or so to seek out and pay for what I need,
And another six minutes to return, ready to go,

Begin or continue my three-hour vigil in the steamy kitchen,
Reveling in the orderly, reasoned process
Of creating, from natural foods, savory sustenance —

A ritual I've performed many times before,
When passing my days as Lake Nebagamon's neighbor,
Reexploring the virtues of an austere existence:

1. Score and dice, with a honed paring knife,
One medium onion.
2. Separate a head of garlic, into its dozen or so cloves,

Cut off their ends, and peel away their papery skin,
Then mince into the tiniest, finest bits.
3. Peel and thinly slice eight to ten carrots.

4. Next, sauté the garlic and onions, in olive oil.
5. Pour in sixty-four ounces of chicken broth,
Before adding carrots, letting them simmer till al dente.

(Discovering that I'm missing the color and texture
Of green and Great Northern beans — two cans each —
I race to Ole's and back, in less than eighteen minutes.)

6. Add four cans of beans; let pot simmer ten minutes.
7. Mix in three quarters of a cup *acini di pepe* pasta,
Which will cook quickly; stir to keep from sticking.

XII. Waves

I've seen this all before — the invasion —
    tens of times, possibly on a hundred occasions,
        in the fall, summer, spring,

Whenever a wild, rebellious, highballing squall
    agitates, aggravates, abrades, exaggerates the waves
        into an unpredictable, quick-changing frenzy,

But never have I seen it like this,
    not any conditions remotely resembling
        the chaotic, rampaging, tumultuous shiftings

Of accumulated dry-powder snow
    being blown, driven, flagellated, by a riled-up wind,
        across the lake's glacial surface —

Glistening cascades of mesmerically drifting flakes
    that could, save for their mercilessly white hue,
        be sand dervishes whirling in a furious desert storm.

Who ever would have thought it possible
    that a body of water so rigid, so somnolent, so immutable
        could spawn waves, in the raw depths of winter?

XI. Sun

This Monday morning, at precisely 7:50,
I was present at the beginning of the sun's manifestation,
Able to record its headfirst birth,

Its emergence from night's uterus, into earthly existence,
Its inexorable rising out of the shore trees, across from me,
Its primordial flaming cries, fiery screams,

Its settling into mothering nature's nurturing arms —
A baby boy she's named "sun,"
Who will bring solace, joy, warmth to this snowy, icy cosmos.

Now, three minutes shy of its diurnal journey's first hour,
The blinding orb is no longer a child, an adolescent,
Rather a man intent on incandescing this land.

X. Snow Spirits

I awaken, this gleaming Sunday in Lake Nebagamon,
To the first sunshine to grace this white country
In five gray days.

The sky is a wondrously laden, broken-open geode,
Exposing its cavernous stratocumulus crystals —
Coruscant, silvery white accreting to the azure.

The iced-over, snow-covered lake is faceted with fire,
Not unlike what I remember being so amazed by,
From mid-May through end-of-September's most recent visits,

And calling "water spirits," as did the Chippewas,
When the sun's pulsating rays struck the breeze-riffled waves,
At the slightest angles of refraction, igniting their tips.

On this golden-orange fourteen-degree morning,
As I sit, half-naked, at the cabin's kitchen table, sipping V8,
Gazing as far as the burning lake takes me,

My senses are dizzy, with these pinpricks of light —
This explosive snow-spirit riot —
And my bones warm, slowly, to their blazing radiance.

IX. Stocking Up

Though snowshoes were useful tools in the woods,
They readily become encumbrances
Once I arrive back at plowed and sanded East Waterfront Drive.

Under the milky halo of a streetlamp
Illuminating the back gate of Camp Nebagamon for Boys,
I bend down, awkwardly, loosen my bindings, and step free,

Commence walking toward the cabin, where I abandon my webs,
And continue on, toward downtown.
How effortless it feels, not to be wearing plaster casts,

Being able to control the strides I take,
Rather than having to lift an entire leg at a time
As if it were static, numb, or I a circus-clown stilt walker.

Now, the village's lamps throw their coppery glows closer together,
As I approach Waterfront Bar & Grill,
Christmas lights festooning its open-for-business aura

And a phalanx of eleven cars parked before it
(Like western-movie horses loosely tied to a saloon's rail),
Greeting all strays who might be out, this breath-catching night.

I keep going, past silent Lawn Beach Inn, the auditorium,
Turn left at the Dairy Queen, head up Lake Avenue,
By busy Bridge's Indianhead Tavern, dark Sharon's Lakeview Cafe,

Chippewa Valley Bank, dentist and post offices, Cable Publishing,
Schaller's Variety Store, Rose's Bakery & Coffee Shop,
Then cautiously cross County Road B, to Ole's Country Market,

A modest grocery store open till eight o'clock.
It's a perfect night for me to stock up on provisions I'm missing:
Lettuce, tomatoes, croutons, broccoli, carrots, red grapes;

Oh, and I mustn't forget to lay in tall kitchen bags,
A jar of peanut butter, a box of crispbread, a ChapStick,
And two or three packages of frozen fish.

All the six-minute walk back to my cabin, over compacted snow,
My visible breath vaporizes, lifts into the bitter-cold sky,
Drifting high, higher, until it mists the yellow, whispering moon.

VIII. A Change in the White Air

By noon, what was left of the tapering flakes had dissipated.
By two, the pervasive white shimmer of sky
Had given way to gray, gray to breaking cloud cover,

Which, by 3:45, when I dressed in my hiking outfit,
Had begun separating into opaque ivory, muted orange, steel blue,
Promising the possibility of an azure twilight.

In my snowshoes, I realized how much better I'm getting
At maneuvering through the woods, above invisible paths,
Which, last summer, I could have scampered along blindfolded.

"Crunch, crunch, crunch," the hard-crusted snow spoke to me,
As I kept growing wearier and heavier, with each step —
Feet, knees, thighs, hips, buttocks pumping, pumping,

Up and down the thick-coated hills of Spitting Spring Trail,
Until, after an hour and a half, my body asked,
"Is all this silent beauty worth it?"

Full-well knowing my answer, before I stopped in my tracks
Just long enough to set such complaints to rest,
Remind my throbbing heart that this was joy in its purest form,

A chance to have these woods and their surrounds all to myself,
Confess to nature, face to face, without reservation,
That I never believed such unadulterated inspiration could exist

Or that I would ever discover such tranquillity in timelessness,
Within such immediacy, just by breathing deeply,
Whenever my spirit is within snowshoeing distance of its soul.

Now, it's 5:15, and as I leave the woods to its placidity,
The setting sun, accompanied by Venus and a waxing-gibbous moon,
Nods at my homeward-bound shadow, as though it knows.

VII. The Blizzard

It began not long before midnight, Wednesday,
And two and a half days later,
The snow has yet to show even the tiniest signs of slowing.

It's still flying around obliquely, vertically,
Transfiguring everything in sight, with its vibrancy,
To the consistent hue of Michelangelo's *David* ground to dust . . .

Everything in this microcosmic universe I alone own,
Here in the unstirring Village of Lake Nebagamon,
Where I've come to celebrate year's end, in my cabin fashion.

To this moment, its been a ubiquitous blur,
Becoming a second flesh the earth will wear for months,
A shapeless white veil draping itself over the abiding land,

Inviting me outside, to traipse in my rawhide-webbed snowshoes,
Meditate on the meaning of Christmas,
Yet lingering over the lake, woods, houses of resilient villagers,

Who, like me, believe that blizzards are necessary blessings
That beckon us to incorporate the sacred rites of winter,
Worship the holy, haloing beauty of blowing snow.

VI. Memory

With no place to go, to be, no one, in particular, to see,
This off-again/on-again-snowy Nativity Friday,
I've gratefully stayed holed up, away from the cold,
Listening to Christmas songs richly recreated
By Barbra Streisand and Nat King Cole,
Wishing that every anyone could be as content as I.

Never have I felt so close to the lake's soul.
The white isolation of its icy silence defines me,
In these hours of sublimely quiet privacy.
Even after tonight and I are tomorrow's memory
And the snow has been reborn as late-April waves,
This memory will be waiting here, to welcome me home.

V. December 25

Long and deep and far past last evening,
The feathery flakes, getting wetter and wetter, fell,
Making the streets treacherous highwaymen.

Frequently, I muddled about, outside,
Not bothered by the elements pelting my hair, my eyes,
While I tried to define the lake, somewhere out there,

Before finally succumbing to weariness,
Disappearing into the slow, serene polar regions of dream-sleep,
As if I too were frozen over, under sheets of ice.

Now, awakened into a renascence, sipping steaming coffee,
I gaze at Lake Nebagamon's southern shoreline
And see the cacophonous wind's voice, hear its shivering touch,

Smell its shrill shape, feel its bracing taste engaging the conifers,
Relieving them of their burdensome weights —
Those snowy ornaments depending from their limbs —

As it shakes them, with fifty-mile-per-hour gusting thrusts,
Freeing them to their untrammeled attitudes.
Doubtless, this will be afternoon's arduous, prolonged mission.

Meanwhile, I have much to accomplish, this Christmas Day,
Verse-gifts to deliver, shadows to meet, old ghosts to visit,
Which are, after all, the reasons I've journeyed here.

But for now — the next solitudinous hours, at least —
At peace with the season, in my cozy, snowbound cabin,
I'll just listen to the wind in the limbs of my mind's pines.

IV. Snowshoeing into Christmas Eve

This exquisite blizzard began at midnight.
Now, another six to eight fluffy inches of powder,
Accumulated on top of the nine or so fallen a week ago,

Make snowshoeing, in full cold-weather gear,
A fantasy begging me to bring it into reality's embrace,
Imploring me to enter the woods, tread on its untainted slate —

The color of Carrara marble — which gives as quicksand does,
Albeit with a grip not nearly so relentless.
My thighs are challenged, retrieving feet, equilibrium,

Just to repeat that sinking sensation leading to painful ecstasy,
Keep me moving through the hushed, ever-green forest
Filled with drooped-bough pines of all varieties.

The only sounds, for millenniums around this emptiness,
Resonate from me, engaging the essence of elemental joy
Emanating from that nexus between spirit and soul.

I stop, to let my lips and tongue sip from a chalice
Held by a white-tufted sprig of a Norway spruce;
The crystallized ichor I taste sates my thirst.

Dusk envelops me long before I notice its descent.
Magical flakes, tumbling through the darkening lattices
Of birches, maples, poplars, oaks, and ashes,

Fill these woods so gradually,
They might be doves escaping the sky's cages.
I'm dazzled by the most unimaginably fluttering wonderment.

Now, the rear gate to the boys' camp,
Where I began, an hour and a half earlier, locates me —
My weary, if completely rejuvenated, silhouette, anyway.

I hate that I've finished my peregrination, for the afternoon,
But Christmas Eve awaits me, at the cabin,
Where the woods — my little tree — will surround me.

III. The Tree

What an exhilarating blood-rush flood it was,
To be back in the woods enwombing the quiet boys' camp,
As I trudged over its snow-packed slopes, in boots.

And now that I'm at the cabin again,
I've one task to get done before I call this afternoon complete
And molt my layers of clothing, take a rest from my labors.

I wade into the west side of the yard descending to the frozen lake,
Saw down a slender, supple, shoulder-high white pine,
Small but perfectly proportioned,

Which will make a fine addition to the living room,
Give that familiar space a strong, sweet scent of Christmas —
A tree all the more festive without lights, ornaments, tinsel.

It's fortuitous that, amidst the basement's dusty clutter,
I locate a rusted red stand, its four green legs intact.
My tiny conifer fits neatly into its grasp.

Having disrobed to my skinny six feet of chilled nakedness,
Finished getting warm, in a soothing, drawn-out shower,
To the core of my blood's gradually quickening flow,

I notice that my tree and I
Are approximately the same height,
Though we're decidedly dissimilar in shape and weight.

More important, we possess something ineluctable,
A mystic trait that binds us, in a brotherly tie,
To the same creative energy — nature the mother to us both.

II. Dressing for the Occasion

Now that I've unpacked my belongings,
Feel fully settled in, for a twelve-day celebration,
I'm eager to explore Lake Nebagamon's snow-draped outdoors.

But I realize I have certain primal desires, unavoidable priorities,
Not the least of which is my need to dress defensively,
In the most appropriate clothing I could buy,

To protect my vulnerable being against the cutting cold,
By insulating its corporeality in the many-layered folds
Of fibers, fabrics, and fillers man-made, plant, and animal.

I bundle up, from toe to torso to shoulders to head:
Knee-length wool stockings; black-silk long underwear;
A second pair of long johns — cotton thermal — over that;

Blue jeans, flannel shirt, and fleece jacket atop them,
Beneath an Arctic-ready, blue, hooded goose-down parka;
Wool cap; neck gaiter; gloves within mittens; lined boots.

How strange it seems, to be so completely cocooned,
Locked inside such a cumbersome second skin,
As though I were a fireman, astronaut, or deep-sea diver,

When, not twelve weeks ago,
I was vigorously walking this village's few main streets
While wearing nothing but jogging shoes, shorts, not even a shirt.

Yet I'm grateful, elated, to be able to withstand this raw blast,
Knowing I *am* a match for its harshest drafts
And that, at will, I can create my own paths, in the woods,

No matter that my feet have to plod in foot-deep snow,
To let me pass through the dense emptiness of naked trees
Decorated, in abstract patterns, by white silence.

But then, isn't it for this, exactly, with unswerving certainty,
That I've returned to this sanctuary, in winter —
To test the limits of my capacity for capturing natural rapture?

I. Back for Christmas

Now, after a five-days-shy-of-three-months lapse,
I'm back in Wisconsin, back in this village, back in my rented cabin,
Back to this earthly source of inspiration I call home,

Whenever my heart petitions me, exhorts me to run away
From the civilized sound, light, air, and mind pollution asphyxiating me,
Escape my numbing humdrum, for a spell of calm.

Though, during my absence, these gorgeous North Woods
Have succumbed to hibernal shapes, shadows, snowy, shivering silences,
I've never seen these purlieus, in their pristine austerity, so beautiful.

I'm mesmerized, elated, ebullient, just being here again,
Breathing in the wintry sky's scintillant, crisp, clean, clear breath,
Trying to acclimatize my listening eyes to the lake's static ice,

When, always, before, they've been beguiled hearing its glistening waves
Ripple against the dock, past the cattail beds, to the shore below my cabin.
Everything's changed so much, and so must I . . . so must I,

If my flesh-and-bones senses intend to surrender, this Christmastide,
To the unforgiving rigors of nature's necessary desolations
And find, in them, the essence of its blessed resurrections.

Christmastide in the Village

XXII. 6:45

Twenty-four hours ago —
At this precise evening time (6:45)
And almost seven hundred miles north of here —

I sat, cross-legged, on a wooden dock,
Watching the blazing sun exit, stage west,
As the quarter moon reflected on the inexorable setting.

Now, those majestic crepuscular seconds,
Which translated their cosmic spell
Into pastel gradations of paradise my eyes recognized,

Have degraded into the city's soul-wracking rataplan,
Abandoning me to abject bereavement,
Causing me to long for nature's nurturing embrace.

I'm sad, to the depths of untold loneliness,
Not to be bedding down, again, in my cozy cabin,
On remote Lake Nebagamon's shores,

Repairing, instead, to my convenience-cluttered condo,
From where, a lifetime of nine nights ago, I left,
In search of lake, loons, sun, moon, and stars.

XXI. Real Tears

All the interminable drive, this Sunday morn,
From Lake Nebagamon to Duluth's airport,
I feel palpable sadness, weep real tears,

Finding myself caught between my recent happiness
And this unhappy vacuum
That's leaving me lower than anything I've known

Since those last moments, four weeks ago,
Which I spent in this tranquil, unhurried land,
Resigned then, as now, to having to go home.

With my visits growing more frequent,
These woefully distressful episodes
Seem to bedevil my spirit more readily, of late.

I'm not quite sure
Just what to make of such shows of emotion,
Why departures keep cutting closer to the heart.

Could it be that mortality is getting the better of me
Or, possibly, that there's yet hope
For my soul to grow, with the water from its tears?

XX. Testament

With the wind gusting off the lake
For the first time in the week I've been here,
Its rough thrusts cutting across my bare chest

And my blood coursing through my throbbing arteries,
As my aching calf and thigh muscles take the steep grades
Of the streets stitching this quiet enclave's existence,

I appreciate my lean body,
The athletic shape I've reclaimed at sixty-eight,
The exhilarating pain I'm experiencing,

In this place that accommodates my need for escape,
And sense that were my time-eliding demise to arrive tonight —
Or right this second, for that black matter —

I'd die a man at the height of his aging's ecstasy,
Satisfied that my bones would know no loneliness,
Resting in the sequestering repose of this village's loam,

That memories of my sweet spirit,
Sojourning here, frequently, over almost sixty years,
Would not be forgotten by the pines, their lake, its loons,

And that my poet's soul would be faithfully reflected
In recitations of my northern Wisconsin testament,
By glory-born sunrises and sunsets.

XIX. Eddie

Toward the end of today's late-morning walk,
Going down the steep hill, to the municipal beach,
Past the "Closed for the Season" Dairy Queen, on my left,
The quiet red-log auditorium, on my right,
I'm lost in thoughts of maintaining this trance indefinitely.

From out of nowhere, a voice calls out my name.
"Is that you? Yes, yes, I recognize you, after all these years!
But I can't really believe I'm seeing you!"
It's my 1954 Camp Nebagamon cabin counselor —
Eddie Drolson, from my summer in Axeman 5 —

A kind man, now in his mid-seventies,
Who helped set my moral compass when I was thirteen.
He seems so happy to find me back in my old clime.
I return his hug, his "I love you,"
And we briefly reprise fifty-five-year-old memories.

He asks what I'm doing in this neck of the North Woods.
I reply that I've been returning, often, to the village,
To write about this land,
Hoping to get a fundamental understanding of who I am,
In relation to who I've been and who I'll be.

Just before I resume my walk, head up the steep hill,
We hug again, smile at each other, say good-bye.
Though I stroll alone, back to my cabin, Eddie is beside me,
Repeating the aphorism he taught me, so long ago:
"Life is too short to be little."

XVIII. Silver and Gold

The silver mist is in an awful hurry, this morning.
I wish I knew where it was off to.
All I can see, from my cabin by the lake,
Is that it's racing, breakneck, across the water,
Like a drunken bum, wearing tattered shrouds,
Stumbling down an eerily lit alley,
Toward somewhere.

All at once, the ten o'clock sun's flaming halo,
Smothered under a wide-hovering cloud cover,
Breaks through, its fire splattering the lake,
Displacing the vapors, with its insistent heat.
They disappear, leaving no traces of the inebriated bum,
Just millions of glistening water spirits —
Gold ripples creating their own mist.

XVII. The Stars

It's a perfectly clear, moonless two o'clock,
And I'm still relaxing out here, at the end of the dock,
Not at all chilled by its fifty-degree subtleties,

Star-watching, stargazing, star-probing,
Through my eyes' amazing telescopes,
Holding the entire cosmos in my own close focus,

Locating and naming all the night sky's constellations,
Conversing with old soul mates, new friends,
Getting to know total strangers.

For the life of my life,
More physically, viscerally, palpably
Than figuratively, metaphorically, even spiritually,

I owe the infinity of stars my every breath.
Without their ancient presences illuminating time,
A vast, black dimension would backlight my somatic space.

XVI. Council Ring

Night's cool breath lingers in the grass's wetness,
Yet I'm perspiring, midway through my spirited walk.
It seems to be wisdom at its most sagacious —
What village folks are saying about summer's having come late.
There's an extra lift in everybody's September-end gait,

Including mine, to be sure,
As I press my unlimber legs not to their breaking point
(Those physical restrictions imposed by aging)
But to their fastest pace,
Knowing that outracing laziness makes the most sense.

Reaching the Council Ring in the noiseless boys' camp,
With its rickety, splintery, unpainted plank benches
And dilapidated, if commanding, totem pole,
Standing, obelisk-like, over the stone-circumscribed firepit,
I decide to deviate from my circuit, slow time down,

Try to take, from this sacred, tree-bowered space,
A few numinous vibrations
Doubtless waiting out here, in this wide, unviolated quiescence,
For me to appropriate, as memories or prophecies,
Possibly both, depending on my powers of conjuration.

Without sensing why,
As if caressingly possessed by spirits of the eighty-one years
Since Camp Nebagamon awakened on these piny shores,
I find myself walking, in measured circles,
Three times counterclockwise, first, then three in reverse —

My whole body a metronome
Keeping beat to symphonies it composed so long ago,
When living was more harmonious, forgiving.
Soon, leaving my circles to their meditations,
I reenter time, backtrack to my cabin,

Relegating my past to its gradually dissipating overtones,
Reacquainting myself with who I am, this minute,
Reveling in feeling the heated soreness in my feet,
The tightness in my calves, the slight ache in my thighs,
My lungs breathing another day through my bloodstream.

XV. Grace

The hundred-fifty-foot, green-limbed white-pine tree
Leaning precariously shoreward, just off my cabin's deck,
Is caw-cawing, with a cohort of eight bellicose crows.
Five crazily calling Canada geese fly by, high.
Wailing loons insinuate the distance, with their primordial chorus.

Silvery mist, this fifty-degree Thursday morning,
Lifts dizzily, sinuously as breath on a cold day,
From each of Lake Nebagamon's warm bays.
And spreading in creamy, opalescent tints, above everything,
Is the yet-unrisen sun's ubiquitous annunciation of its coming.

What's missing from this tableau approximating Genesis
I needn't ask myself; I already know. It's me.
To complete this scene, I have to make my relevance felt,
Define and posit my raison d'être,
A quintessential sense of consequence, to proclaim my presence.

But what that might possibly be, I'm not altogether certain,
Lest it have everything to do
With whether this rendition of Creation gets written down,
Passed on, as a reminder, to mankind's generations,
That our place in nature is defined by imagination's grace.

XIV. Masterpiece

Have you ever seen a lake change colors,
Transmute its normal translucent hues
To the holy roses, yellows, golds, and oranges
Cimabue, Giotto, and Masaccio used,
To decorate the sacred flesh of their Renaissance frescoes?

I did, this cool, northern Wisconsin Wednesday night,
After the sun departed the July-like day,
Its comet-tail brush painting,
In the wake of its fading away,
The glorious dabs and strokes of its celestial masterpiece.

XIII. Two Geese

It's 6:45. A crescent moon has lifted,
Visibled itself, in the cloudless, yet-blue sky,
High above the shadow-gathering trees across from me.

A rose-orange twilight sun is descending fast,
About to make its ceremonial exit, beyond Lorber Point,
Into Lake Nebagamon's western bay, near Minnesuing Creek.

Two honking Canada geese, flying in graceful tandem,
Are headed in the sun's direction,
As if to witness its dying flames set the trees ablaze.

At dock's end, sensing the water's serenity,
I've begun to understand what day's finality means,
When the sun's energy, if never spent, is suspended

Until the commencement of dawn's yawning light.
Now, it's night's turn to revitalize earth's creatures.
Sleep needs time, to work its healing.

The crescent moon is higher, brighter.
The sky has dimmed to a muted chalky haze.
The same two honking geese are flying over me, easterly.

XII. Southern-Shore Odyssey

Getting a way-too-late start on this midweek day,
For letting the water spirits on Chequamegon Bay
Fascinate me into protracted contemplation of native lore,

I hastily dress in jeans, flannel shirt, hiking shoes.
Determined to make my return journey to Lake Nebagamon
A modern-day odyssey,

I begin at Gruenke's, in downtown Bayfield,
With three blueberry pancakes, syrup, steaming decaf,
Then head south, along Lake Superior, to Washburn,

Where I buy *Loon Magic*, at Chequamegon Books,
Stop at Coco, to purchase a baguette,
Then drive back north, to the orchards above Bayfield.

Arriving at Blue Vista Farm, I set about picking Redfrees —
Two half bushels, weighing twenty pounds each —
Which I intend, come Saturday, to make into applesauce.

With my fruit stashed securely in the car's trunk,
I'm off again, easterly, toward unincorporated Cornucopia,
A village on Siskiwit Bay's sandy shore,

Boasting a modest marina, a boat-repair facility,
Halvorson Fisheries, O'Bryon's and Fish Lipps restaurants,
And Ehlers early-twentieth-century general store,

Offering hardware, groceries, deli items,
Where I pay for a small plastic tub of homemade hummus,
Which I, once settled by the water, spread on my artisan bread,

Before resuming my drive, for another forty-five minutes,
And reaching the dirt road leading to the mouth of the Brule,
Flowing slowly into the mother of all freshwater lakes.

By this time, a palette of twilight is at my back.
I climb down the dunes, to the rocky beach, admire the wilds,
Watch a great blue heron wade along the river's banks,

Foraging, with primeval precision, for its afternoon catch.
By 5:45, I'm back at my cabin,
Glad to have had a brief retreat from my brief retreat.

XI. Acorns

Fall is the tepid gusts
Rustling the oak trees' leaves above me,
Snapping acorns from their limbs,
Which cause a plangent commotion
As they plummet earthward,
Disturbing attendant silences,
Pelting the Winfield Inn's porch roof,
Relentlessly thumping the ground —
Explosions nobody around this shoreline
Can possibly miss,
Even if they're not listening.
After all, fall *is* all about falling.

X. Water and Fire

By nine, the sun's spitting acetylene-torch tip
(Burning an invisible fissure into the pristine sky,
From below its initial treetop incision,
Along Lake Superior's southern shore,
To high over the Apostle Islands archipelago)

Has left a dazzlingly faceted cascade of brilliance,
In a controlled, molten flow of yellow heat,
Across Chequamegon's north channel,
From Madeline Island to Bayfield,
Above whose bustle I've stayed the night, at peace.

Now, unable to keep a bead on the torch's light-source,
I examine the gash it's cut across the bay's expanse
And marvel at how paradoxes like this can exist —
That water and fire need each other, to breathe,
As much as I need them, to water and fire my being.

IX. Amateur Naturalist

How elementally comforting it is,
Awakening to rain reciting, to me, its proverbs and psalms,
Just beyond my cabin's open windows,

And knowing I've not yet taken time to decide
Whether I'll go to the only place I have to be going:
Nowhere.

In any event, I'll either stay holed up
Or manage to walk in and around, up and down, the town
And along the sand-path labyrinths of the closed boys' camp.

Now, the precipitation seems to have taken shelter elsewhere
Or, like an ancient geyser, played itself out;
Either way, the afternoon belongs to me.

Outdoors, doing my warmup stretches,
I'm engulfed in a low-hovering, cloud-laden mist,
An ash-white circumambience of dense saturation,

As though what, just hours ago, was a steady downpour
Has escaped into a vaporous state,
Chosen to suspend its peremptory intentions indefinitely,

Content to have left its legacy of wetness
Dripping from tree leaves, glistening on grass,
Gathered in street puddles, gutters, on every tangible surface.

Ah, but then, wouldn't you know it,
Just when I think we're all done with today's changes
And I've ranged half a mile away from my cabin,

Here comes the chilly rain, again,
Playing me for the amateur naturalist I'll always be,
Unable to read creation's most elemental elements.

VIII. My Own Cosmos

Still settled here, at 11:15, on the dock's-end bench,
This mid-sixty-degree Monday evening,
Listening to crickets chirping in the near distance,

Craning my neck heavenward,
To survey the stars in the amorphous Milky Way,
Their fluctuating, diamond-dust constellations

Weaving the sky's hundred billion galaxy-threads
Into a spectacular astral tapestry of interstellar space,
I understand just how fortunate my aging spirit is,

To experience this privilege of years,
In which I'm yet able to see luminous bodies aligning
Above this northern Wisconsin seclusion,

With one occasionally falling from the sky,
Landing in my eyes, like a dandelion-parachute vision,
Exhorting me to incorporate it into the crickets' songs.

VII. Face to Face

I've been up since well before sunrise,
Measuring the weather, scouting out clouds,
Counting the lake's metered waves,
Chipmunks and squirrels scurrying,
Spiders, flies, moths, gnats, ants, and bees stirring,
Noting the lack of mosquitoes, geese, loons,
Tracking red maple leaves, to record their destinations.

This enthralling, fall-mocking seventy-degree afternoon,
Seven hours past day's immaculate break,
I have no doubt, at all,
That nowhere else exists.
How could it, conceivably, for someone like me,
Who's gazed deep into these immortal North Woods
And seen nature's face, face to face?

VI. Early-Afternoon Swim

Lunch, this sunny Monday,
Is yesterday's sumptuous homemade salmagundi soup
(Vegetable broth loaded with olive oil and garlic,
A richly textured admixture of Great Northern beans,
Chunky tomatoes, zucchinis, carrots,
And a generous portion of *acini di pepe* pasta),
Then fresh raspberries, blackberries, strawberries.

Next, I wander from my cabin, to the shore,
In nothing but my red jogging shorts,
And wade into the lake's sensual embodiment,
As if making slow, sweet, voluptuous love to it.
Its labial shallows envelop me, in their fluid element,
Impel me to penetrate deeper,
Exhort me to seek release, ecstasy, in its warm core.

Having walked a hundred feet out
And still not gotten my head, let alone chest, wet,
I immerse myself beneath the surface.
How refreshed, cleansed, purified my entire body feels —
Revitalized, energized, stimulated, young again,
As I was when only ten, at the boys' camp,
During "General Swim"s, in this very same water.

And though that was fifty-eight summers ago,
I do know that yesteryear and today
Are, inseparably, one and forever more,
Just as tomorrow will always be this very shore,
Below this warm, comforting cabin,
Beckoning me to dive into Lake Nebagamon,
Embrace it as it embraces me — inspired lovers.

Directly across the lake's surface,
From its seat in the eastern reaches, to me,
Seated here, by myself, in mesmerized silence,
On the end of this dock,
Knowing that if I so choose,
I can climb that swath, into the sky —
All the way from right here to the horizon,
Where the sun is burning off the clouds —
Without my disappearing into the dark side of day.

7:15 A.M.

Five minutes later,
Though the eastern bay of Lake Nebagamon
Is bathed in layers of ivory, gold, pink, and orange,
The furiously blazing ball
Is hidden within the overshading of gray welkin.

The quiet, dynamic sky is regal,
Suffused with a solemn dignity no one can know,
Who never ventures out of sleep,
To see, feel, intimately, his small piece of Earth
Come awake, come alive, come closer to eternity.

V. Monday Sunrise

6:30 A.M.

Morning starts at night's dark margins,
Giving up, grudgingly, its gray nocturnal privacy,
To widening striations of red, orange, and white,
Just above the eastern peaks of maples, oaks, and pines,
In the vicinity of Bumble's Bay.

The only sounds, for miles of shadowy shore around,
Are the caw-caw-cawings of crows,
Five of which, midlake and high, in formation,
Are chasing a pair of frantically honking Canada geese.
Soon, two bald eagles fly overhead, sunrise bound.

Now, the stratus cover has begun to dissipate,
While the sun comes inching into sight.
I watch, with rapt and awed amazement,
As that orange sphere ignites —
A fire raging at the edges of a cloud-enshrouded prairie.

Within seconds, a majestic spectrum of brightening light
Paints the space above the bay, with glory.
The radiant star breaks through,
Proclaims itself lord of the morning sky.
Witnessing its coronation, I shiver, from its heat.

7:00 A.M.

The price of admission to daybreak
Is just wishing to bear witness,
Then being here, on this dock,
At the anointed minute —
Commencement of the sun's ascension.

7:10 A.M.

Within ten minutes,
The dazzling corona has risen high enough
To cast its brilliant orange swath
*

IV. Pontoon Plane

For a too-brief interlude,
This infinitely quiet Saturday afternoon,
The drone of a single-engine pontoon plane
(Circling the lake's perimeter, three times,
To assess whatever surface traffic might be occurring,
The direction of its prevailing breezes)
Only heightens the silence of this day, for me.

I'm conscious of the plane's intrusion into this air space,
If for no other reason than that it awakens me
To the contemporaneous nature of grace,
Makes me aware of just how precious serenity is,
Especially when it's wrested from our expectations,
After we've descended into the smugness that arises
When we rely on what comes without cost.

Soon, I hear the plane growing louder,
As it goes slower, lower, closer to the water's runway,
Heading into the wind blowing northerly,
Out of the bay, where the YMCA camp slumbers.
Then it turns. My ears detect the engine winding,
Driving that yellow, silver-winged bird
Toward where I'm standing, on the shore below my cabin.

Instead of finding a dock and stopping the prop,
The invisible pilot maneuvers the plane into another one-eighty,
Until it's facing southerly, its engine roaring,
Its tiny body racing across the mild chop, lifting, lifting,
Lumbering over Honeymoon Point,
Trailing its low drone behind it, like an ad banner,
Rising just over the trees, higher, veering left,

Out of sight, its lingering roar growing soft, softer,
Then, not five minutes later, reverberant once more,
As it descends again, not fifty feet above my cabin,
Unnerving my bones, making another deft landing.
Suddenly, the pontoon plane is gone forever,
Leaving Saturday afternoon's quietude to my keeping.
I can't wait to see what the lake and I decide to do with it.

III. Quiet Saturday in Lake Nebagamon

It's almost two thirds of the way through September,
Yet the trees, save for sugar maples and wild sumacs
(The first to display red shades of decay),
Remain boastful, haughty, you might say,
In their vibrant-green defiance of autumnal change.

Though a golden-glowing warmth pervades this village —
Nearly eighty unseasonable degrees —
No boaters, skiers, fishermen, seeking relaxation,
Are roiling the lake's surface,
Leaving dizzying hurly-burly in their wakes.

This calm suits me just fine,
Allows me solitude unviolated by human doing —
The peace I've come here seeking, hoping to find,
To mine from this clime's abundant stores of the sublime,
And translate into psalms my mind might recite.

Not even bothering to lock my cabin door,
I step out onto the deck, into a brilliant morning,
Wearing only shorts, socks, jogging shoes,
And, in a heightened state of low-key excitement,
Set off walking about the town, at an energized gait.

Soon, I slip into a meditative state of invisibility,
Quickly outdistance not the limitations of time and place
But the issues of who I am, why I exist, what's next,
Which assail me, daily, even at sixty-eight,
When I'm back in the city, watching clocks tock and tick.

However many life spans long an hour really is,
That's what it takes me to complete my circuit,
Return refreshed, disrobe, shower, shave,
Assume my blue-jean-and-plaid-flannel identity, again,
And savor Saturday's quiescence, for the rest of my destiny.

II. Whispering

This brisk Friday evening,
In these first hours of my people's New Year,
The beginning of the High Holy Days — Rosh Hashanah —

So far away from St. Louis, my place of birth,
I feel wholly at home, reborn to who I'm meant to be,
I a Jew no matter however so nominally,

However so reformed, however so negligible,
An assimilated shadow of my Mosaical shadow,
Who's strayed very too far away from my heritage.

Here, I'm free to choose my house of worship — the stars —
Under whose roof I'll pray,
Without feeling guilty for not attending temple,

Free to heed nature's voice, not YHWH's,
And acknowledge that, though a minor light among His chosen,
I hold, within my soul, the power to alter the cosmos,

As I wander in my own Promised Land —
This sacred place of patriarchal pine trees and lakes.
Just now, I hear them whispering, *"l'shana tova."*

I. This Moment

Let me mark this September moment,
Register this glorious Lake Nebagamon dusk,
In the majestical key of free-verse poetry,
So that I won't ever forget
How euphoric I feel, this Friday night,
In the hollow of my bones, my blood's crimson,
My chromosomes, my spirit's holiest of souls.

What I'd like to record,
Here on Lawn Beach Inn's wraparound deck,
Overlooking the lake as it looks up at me,
With the sun lifting its pastel-red embers,
Even as it descends,
Scattering them across this twilight sky,
Is a mad, passionate howl exceeding my rapture,

If only I could capture a synthesis of nature,
From man's most ancient wisdom,
Its signs, symbols, myths, visions, dreams,
With an entirely organic vocabulary
Expressing elation, ecstasy.
But I balk, stutter, grope for adequate imagination
With which to recreate this Wisconsin eve.

Now, when my eyes rise from my meditations,
Nothing's left of the sunset.
Venus beams amidst gossamer darkness.
Though cold, at this fifty-degree moment,
I radiate jubilation, just being able to sit here
And gaze at this wordless sky,
Reflected in this unloquacious lake.

Sunrises and Sunsets

Once just beyond the dock, the flock wheels again,
Into the drifting mist, then turns, midlake, and faces me.
They descend, lower and lower, until each has landed.

The stark silence is astonishing — not a sound from them,
No noise on the calm lake,
Nothing, that is, save one lone loon's solo tremolo.

No more than fifty yards from them, shivering, I listen, watch.
The vapor begins to dissipate,
Disappear into the sun rising, lifting, climbing inexorably,

Until, within minutes, seconds, timeless epiphanies,
I notice that nothing's left of the gossamer mist,
And in its place are the lake's glistening, barely rippling sheen,

Twenty-three geese (floating peacefully, now, in a line),
And me, transfixed on the dock —
All of us inextricably integral to this Wisconsin tableau.

XXIII. Morning Mist

It's 6:30 a.m.
What am I doing up so early,
This still, chill-shrouded Sunday — my last few hours here?

I have to believe that *something* made me awaken,
Because I've preempted my alarm clock's call
By a whole half-hour.

Staring out the kitchen window, at the lake's placidity,
I'm beguiled by a rolling, low-drifting mist.
Silver-white and hovering just above the water,

It seems to be emanating out of Bumble's Bay,
To the east of my cabin.
I want, desperately, to witness the pine-blocked sunrise.

Suddenly, barefoot, in nothing but my briefs,
I'm outside, on the deck, down the slippery stairs,
In the wet, cold grass leading to the colder, wetter wooden dock.

Now, I can witness the sun
Unveil itself from the scattering haze,
Pour its flaming-orange lava down the sky's corridor.

To the south of me, in the direction of Honeymoon Point,
I hear a crazy, clattering chatter of Canada geese
And locate them high above the trees, flying away,

Toward Minnesuing Creek, on the lake's westernmost bay.
Then, all that noise filling the blue — their wild honking —
Coalesces into the flock coming, in a full-wheeling tilt,

Steadily toward me, as a majestical, undulating V,
Where I'm standing, at dock's end.
They must see me, want me to see them, in their exuberance.

Before I can finish counting all those huge, looming birds,
They're directly overhead, low enough, almost, to touch.
It's as if they want to show me something.

XXII. Eight Nights and Days

When you live in a busy city,
Spending eight nights and days
In a remote place
Like the village of Lake Nebagamon
Is a contentment of eternities.

For that matter,
Were the eight nights and days
Abridged by a whole week,
Being here would still be
The sweetest lifetime conceivable.

XXI. Loons and Crows

An old patrician male loon I've seen here, for years,
Gracefully glides across the tranquil water,
Dives, resurfaces, forages again,
Between my cabin and Camp Nebagamon's back gate,
Letting everyone know, for myriad miles around,
With its echoing yodels, tremolos, hoots, and wails,
That it alone owns the whole lake.

And who am I,
On my Saturday-morning walk around this slumberous town,
Up and down its few main and side streets,
To argue such presumptuous claims to suzerainty?
Indeed, I'd be all for a hegemony of common loons
Ruling over this community of a thousand souls,
Be satisfied to respect the laws of the land it might set.

Soon, I come upon a dead maple tree, in an empty lot,
Clotted with a black confederation of five ungainly crows
Cawing raucously, vituperatively,
Daring me to stop them from rifling a nearby trash container.
I can't miss the detritus they've strewn on the sidewalk:
Ketchup, plastic cups, napkins, French fries.
They seem to be plotting a takeover of the entire village.

For seconds, I ponder the implications of such plundering,
Then continue undaunted,
Aware that the rites of Lake Nebagamon's loons and crows
Don't come under my purview, jurisdiction.
They have a pressing responsibility to sustain themselves —
Just as I do, on my strenuous walks,
Feeding my body's and spirit's need to maintain, maintain.

XX. Lovers

This yet-blue low-sixties twilight,
I sit by myself, outdoors, at Lawn Beach Inn,
Watching two rambunctious teenagers —

The only swimmers at the municipal beach.
After a few minutes, they climb atop the anchored raft,
The girl in a skimpy bikini, the boy in baggy trunks,

Both cavorting, holding each other close,
Repeatedly caressing, kissing, unabashedly,
Oblivious of anyone who might be looking at them.

By the time I pour a glass of wine and gaze out again,
The adolescents are gone; the raft is abandoned;
And I'm as alone as I was when I first sat down,

Though not lonely,
Since I have my own companion beside me, tonight.
The lake and I have been lovers, for ages.

XIX. Rap-Rap-Rapping

My walk through the abandoned campgrounds,
This luminous Friday afternoon, is necessarily slow and short
(My legs are weary, sore, from this morning's hike);
Nonetheless, it's eventful, scintillant, inspiring,
For the sun shafts dappling the trees, with shadowy silence.

Having passed by the desolate waterfront area,
Now stacked, every which way, with docks, canoes, rowboats,
I arrive in the Axeman Village,
Drawn, hauntingly, to a drum-tap rap-rap-rapping
Calling me to its source, as if with an urgent message.

Only, when I locate what turns out to be a pileated woodpecker,
Tapping tenaciously, at a defenseless forty-foot maple,
With its hammerlike red-crested head, powerful, sharply pointed bill,
Its long, muscular neck the tool's handle,
All I can do is stand silent, mesmerized, looking directly up,

As I'm showered with white chips and yellowish chunks
That land in my hair, on my shirt.
I'm not certain if this surprisingly large bird notices or cares I'm here,
For its being so invested in digging insects, from bark, hardwood,
Ingesting them almost as fast as it can remove new layers.

For half an hour, until I grow dizzy, gazing skyward,
I watch this master sculptor chisel away, at its wood block,
Creating, if not an intricate piece of abstract art,
At least an approximation of a primal design
And leaving behind its signature, to designate its handiwork.

Even as I take to the spongy pine-needle paths, again,
My footfalls diminishing into the accumulating distance,
I can still hear that woodpecker disturbing the atmosphere,
With its drum-tap rap-rap-rapping, and I'm a happy man,
For having spied on and been inspired by such dedication to work.

XVIII. Family Campers

Two days ago,
This season's alumni and their families
Said their final good-byes
To Camp Nebagamon, for boys of all ages,
Cut their evanescent ties with nature's humble ways,
And headed back into their busy, insulated lives,
In Chicago, St. Louis, Los Angeles, New York.

Only I, who hadn't participated
In the weeklong Family Camp program
(Guaranteed to evoke memories, green and golden,
Of those summer yesterdays of old),
Remained behind,
To survey the camp's closing down,
Record the fleet dismantling of the palpable magic

That insinuates itself, nine weeks each summer,
Into what, otherwise, is just a hodgepodge of cabins,
A catchall for sailboats, docks, patched canoes,
Tennis rackets, baseball bats and gloves,
Ramshackle rituals and myths
Recycled, since 1929, as if they were gospel . . .
Which, somehow, they are.

Now, under an invigorating drizzle,
I walk, at a meditative pace, over the sodden sandy paths,
And say hello to the pervasive emptiness,
Grateful that this place is sacred to me, as well.
Suddenly, I know why I'm still here:
My own Family Camp is in full swing;
The man and the boy I am are becoming friends again.

XVII. The Clouds and the Stars

Could it be that the clouds are more numerous than the stars?
Who can make that determination? Not I.
I deal strictly in the numinous, the metaphysical, the poetic.

A meteorologist, an astronomer, I'm not.
I'm best at describing a lake, like the one before me,
At just the second it catches a charge of sunrays

Breaking through a blue interstice amidst the scud,
In a pervasively fluffy overlay of black/gray/white striations
Conspiring, with the sky, to rob Earth of its light . . .

Best at detecting water spirits flashing across rippling waves,
Speaking, to me, in their untranslatable native tongues,
Each refracting facet reciting an epic my soul knows by heart —

Or is it my heart knows by soul?
Either way, nature and I cherish our ongoing dialogue;
It's the only way the two of us can keep in touch with my humanity.

And now I recognize that what's infinitely more crucial to me
Than assigning a number to the stars, the clouds,
Is just taking the time to change places with the sky.

XVI. Anything Goes

This gray, rain-drizzled day,
Lunch is as easy as heating up a panful of angel-hair pasta,
Savoring the marinara sauce I concocted, last evening.

Within minutes, I'm in business. Now, I'm fully sated.
Mopping up the remainder of the red gravy on my plate,
With fresh-cut slices of Italian bread, I contemplate the afternoon —

Whether I'll stay in, read one of the dozen books I've brought,
Or go out, on the end of the dock,
Let myself get wet, to the flesh, the bone, the marrow, the soul.

Possibly, if I choose to keep warm, indoors,
I'll watch a movie or listen to music.
What's nice is that it's all up for grabs — anything goes.

And who knows? I just might compose an ineffable poem
About how, before I ever became a lake,
I apprenticed as rain, falling, for days, in northern Wisconsin.

I then boiled water, in another pot, shaking in two teaspoons of salt,
And, in the final minutes (the last six, to be exact),
Dropped in all fourteen and a half ounces of angel-hair pasta.

When it was done, I drained it and stirred in the sauce,
Transferred dinner to a large bowl, which I brought to the table,
Then served myself the first of three platefuls of steaming delight,

Along with a green salad and thin-sliced Italian bread,
And the evening was complete.
This morning, I know what I'll have for breakfast: these aromas.

XV. Aromas

The yawning, awakening cabin
Is yet bathed in the aromas of last evening's cooking —
The sweet marinara sauce I made, from scratch.

Had you seen the *joie de vivre* dancing in my eyes,
You'd have thought I fancied myself a world-class chef,
As I meticulously prepared those carefully chosen ingredients

And incorporated them, one by one,
Into the eight-quart pot among the kitchen's amenities —
Dicing, mincing, slicing, scissoring, chopping, grating,

Getting slowly, ebulliently lost in the expanding fragrances
Lifting from the old electric stove,
Into every crevice, niche, and fiber of this cozy habitation.

Indeed, I was so absorbed in the steps of my recipe,
I never stopped to ask why I was so impassioned,
Rather just kept feeding my passion's appetite:

1. Add a couple tablespoons of olive oil; heat till hot;
2. Cut off ends of ten garlic cloves; peel skin; mince; throw in;
3. Mince as many green onions as possible, more; toss in;

4. Add tomato puree, preferably three pints;
5. Follow up with two small cans of tomato paste;
6. Stir in one pint diced tomatoes;

7. Now, the secret to it all: one-half cup Beaujolais-Villages;
8. Add one-half teaspoon salt — just a smidgen;
9. Sprinkle in one-eighth teaspoon, approx., of pepper;

10. Cut up, with scissors, one teaspoon oregano leaves fresh off stalk;
11. Ditto with leaves of garden-plucked basil — two tablespoons;
12. Grate one-half cup Asiago cheese; sprinkle into the sauce.

After an hour of elated fascination with the process,
I stirred the simmering, thickening "gravy," with my wooden spoon,
Every fifteen minutes, for the next two hours.

XIV. Lazy Day

Here in Lake Nebagamon,
It's been raining for twenty-four hours.
Remaining in the cabin has been a full-time occupation,
A joy, really, with nothing better for me to do
Than listen to the precipitation drip onto the deck
And watch its steady progress,
As it perforates the lake's surface, with its gentle pellets.

When I was a camper, nearby, fifty-odd years ago,
We called a gray, wet break in the busy season, like this,
A "lazy day," which signaled a rare chance to sleep in,
Followed by a visit to the rec hall, between 8:30 and 10:00,
To have a buffet of eggs (any style), bacon, buttered toast —
A far cry from the usual milk/cereal/K.P.-duty breakfast,
Followed by a double-session of morning/afternoon projects.

Occasionally, it's a privilege, indulging in a nothing-to-do day,
Juggling a time-on-my-hands a.m. and p.m.,
Just for the sake of letting the world be, without me.
In this slowly disclosing moment of perfect equanimity,
I can only hope that the rain keeps poking holes
In the lake's calm expanse,
Letting me know all's well, with my soul's steady progress.

XIII. Blueberry Afternoon

This bracing Wednesday a.m.,
Chequamegon Bay and its surrounds
Form a vibrant still life
In yellow, green, gray-white, and silver —
Yarrow plants interlacing ubiquitous sumac
And leafy birch and maple trees,
Argenteous sky and lake mirroring each other.

Soon, the day will be overlaid with dark blue —
Blueberries I'll pick, at Blue Vista Farm,
In the acres of orchards perched above Bayfield,
And take back with me, to Lake Nebagamon,
Northlands and Patriots in pint boxes
And on my fingertips, lips, and tongue . . .
That taste of blue lingering all afternoon.

XII. Each Other's Shadows

Leaving the village of Lake Nebagamon, I reach Brule,
Then follow the southern shore of Lake Superior,
Through Port Wing, Herbster, Cornucopia,

Arrive, an hour and a quarter later, in Washburn,
Before homing in on Bayfield,
Where I'll spend the night, at the Winfield Inn,

In a room, high on a hill, overlooking the lake —
A placid sweep of Chequamegon Bay,
Facing Madeline Island.

Now that I'm here and settled in,
I know that the lake's been following me, and I it;
We're each other's shadows.

Sometimes, like right this very lifetime of mine,
When our affinities coincide so intimately,
I'm certain that, once, I was a lake.

XI. In My Bones

This Tuesday, at daybreak,
I decide a vigorous hike would be a boon to my bones,
Let them shake the frigidity from their marrow —

A march through the village's quiet downtown,
Then into the boys' camp,
Still hosting, the entire week, fifty or so alumni families,

Before it shuts down tight, for its protracted hibernation.
Outside the cabin, I stretch my sinews and muscles,
Then set off, on my jaunty walk,

Trying to forget, if not reject, the wind's insistence,
So filled with a sharp chill
That it razors through my jogging shorts, fleece jacket.

But within minutes, my whole body grows warm, jubilant,
Invites me to revel in its finely tuned movements.
I'm precision clockwork fully wound, calibrated to ecstasy.

For an hour, lost in my stream of timeless consciousness,
I exult in the lake, the trees, the houses passing me by,
The sky, which never lets me out of its sight.

Striding quickly, fluidly, I know, in my bones,
That I'd rather be right here, going nowhere, everywhere,
Than anywhere else, going everywhere, nowhere.

X. Open Windows

An exhilarating chill fills my cabin, this early morning.
The outdoors took its cue, last evening,
When I welcomed it in, to sleep with me.

It was a simple sign we'd arranged between us:
If I felt so inclined, I'd leave all my windows open,
Which I did, before climbing into dreams.

Now, the thermometer outside the kitchen window reads fifty-six.
The sun's up; the sky's blue;
The lake, flowing angularly to the shore, is rippled.

I can tell this is going to be another scintillating day,
Though my icy bones and goose-pimpled flesh,
Shivering visibly, have yet to warm to the prospect.

Sipping steaming decaf, from a double-thick mug,
I recall how, in my Wisconsin-summering youth,
I'd spend two months at a time, at Camp Nebagamon,

Where I and my mates, in our uninsulated cabins,
With only canvas tarps covering the screened windows,
Would have called last evening a "three-blanket night."

Perhaps I still crave these frigid wake-up visitations
Because they reconnect me with another me,
Relocate both of us in the flow of life.

Maybe this is why, when I'm here and the air is nippy,
I leave all the windows open, go to bed,
Hoping the cold will hold me close, under the covers.

IX. Clocking In

It's barely 6:45,
On this cloudless, cerulean Monday dawn,
Yet I've already punched metaphor's time clock,
On the end of this wet, wood-planked dock.
Even now, the sun has noted my arrival.

Across the water,
Toward the old YMCA camp in the south bay,
A loon lets loose a flurry of worried tremolos.
In the giant white pine tilting, severely,
Just below my cabin's kitchen door,

Boisterous crows — five or eight, at least —
Are too busy dominating this early hour,
With their abrasive calls and responses, to notice me;
Perhaps they imagine themselves Chanticleers,
With the fabled duty of waking the lake's kingdom.

And here I sit, amidst this crisp Wisconsin breeze,
Listening to the rhythmic waves
Performing their subtle dance, against the sandy shore,
Realizing I've only got the whole day to make a poem
From nothing but everything surrounding me.

VIII. Lives

At 8:30, the sun having yet to set,
I'm the lone guest on Lawn Beach Inn's deck,
Whose towering trees, in sympathy with the breezes,
Whisper gentle rhapsodies, to my contentment.
Sunday evening is reluctant to leave Lake Nebagamon.

Gazing at the public beach, below,
I watch the last brave souls emerge from the cold water,
Dry off, with oversize towels, don night's robe,
And I speculate on the lives awaiting them,
Anticipate the life waiting for me,

When I finish eating, walk back to my cabin,
Where I've known happiness, for days, weeks, on end,
Over the past four years,
The life I leave up here, reluctantly, each time I pack,
Head home, to the life that keeps sending me back.

VII. Clouds

Hanging around the lake, this Sunday,
I've taken my peaceful time, just counting clouds
As they pass, on their way to wherever they're going.

They've not seemed too lazy, or eager either,
To rendezvous with their destinations,
But indefatigable, persistent, resolute, free,

As though knowing the coordinates they need
To reach some predestined locus
Beyond the tree-lined horizon holding my focus.

Even now, they're scudding right into twilight,
Above, yet under, my tired, scrutinizing eye;
I've been keeping tabs since dawn, and now I'm weary.

Although I've numbered hundreds, thousands of clouds,
They show no signs of dissipating,
And I wonder how many more there are to come,

How many days I'd have to spend, counting them,
How many lifetimes my mind would require,
To record their inexorable migration, from beginning to end.

VI. Cattails

Forty-mile-per-hour gusts
Are creating tumultuous waves, on the glistening lake,
Thrusting them, aslant, toward the besieged shore.

From the end of this ruggedly buffeted dock,
Looking back up, at my cabin,
I watch the vast stand of lush-green, flower-spiked cattails

Bend, against this irrepressible force of nature,
Like cornstalks and milo in a violent prairie storm.
I'm amazed by how pliant their viridescent stems are,

Many of them seven, eight feet tall
(Not counting the foot or so that's underwater).
The four volunteer willows, growing in their midst,

Take a brutal lashing, too,
As do the three-foot-high yellow-blossoming yarrow plants,
Creeping up to their margins, from the sandy land.

There's something ominous about these bulrushes
That causes my imagination apprehension.
They seem almost invasive, poised to take over the shore.

Now, I'm thinking that I'd be quite happy
Were this wind to continue until it flattens these cattails,
Lets the lake reclaim what they've rapaciously seized.

Who enlisted, at twenty-one, in the Army Air Corps,
Survived to boast forty kills — more than any other pilot, ever —
Only to die testing Lockheed's experimental P-80 jet, in 1945.

Now, making the short drive back to my lakeside cabin,
All I can think is how heroic Major Bong was
And how fortunate I am, to have flown his plane.

V. Historical Marker

During my first few summers at Camp Nebagamon for Boys
(When I was ten, eleven, twelve —
Not all that many years after World War II),

On Cruiser Days or other occasional breaks in the daily routine,
My cabin and village mates and I
Would be bused to Poplar, a mere nine miles away, on Highway 2,

To see a strange-looking vintage fighter plane
(Stranded in a patch of scratchy weeds, just off the highway)
Designated "Historical Marker."

I can still recall climbing all over that dilapidated aircraft's wings,
Grasping its props, crawling into the canopyless cockpit,
Its dashboard lacking most of the knobs, toggles, instruments —

A vandalized relic from the war before the Korean Conflict,
A derelict monument to some guy with the weird name of "Bong,"
A pilot, from the local area, who died.

And that was the extent of the significance my incurious mind
Brought to that symbol rotting in the middle of nowhere,
The monumentality of that scrap-metal junk,

Until today, when I drove from Lake Nebagamon,
Up P, to 2, then west, past Poplar, in seconds,
Toward the Perkins restaurant in Superior,

Located next to a sleek museum dedicated in 2002 —
The Richard I. Bong Veterans Historical Center,
In which, after finishing lunch, I decided to invest an hour.

Once inside, I stood in awe of a twin-engine fighter plane
Identical to the one that had been "stationed" in Poplar —
A completely restored Lockheed P-38 Lightning,

Sporting a color portrait of Bong's gal, Marge, on its nose,
Just beside twenty-five painted Japanese flags, designating kills . . .
Stood eye to eye, with that intimidating machine . . .

Stood in the aura of that Congressional Medal of Honor recipient,
Who'd grown up on his parents' farm, in Poplar,
With eight siblings and a passionate childhood dream of flying,

IV. Grown-Up Boys

I had so hoped that this sojourn in Lake Nebagamon
Would coincide with the last few days of the second-four-weekers
And I'd be able, during walks around my former haunts,
To catch glimpses of the boys at final projects,
Who'd remind me of those glorious summers of my coming of age.

But to my disappointment,
They've already departed; family camp has begun,
The cabins filled with spouses and children primed for fun,
Grown-up boys eager to recreate that magical time
When everything was larger than life, not diminished by hindsight.

On today's energized, five-mile, hour-and-a-half walk,
I pass in and out of my stomping grounds twice,
Witness, from a distance, the adults gathered for happy hour,
Cordially conversing, fondly reminiscing, laughing.
I think I may recognize a few of them.

Then I slip away, over a secluded, shadowy path,
Back into my spirited clip, beyond the gate, toward town,
Glad for not having had to engage in small talk about the past —
My most private shrine,
Where only my soul and the grown-up boy in me come to worship.

III. Dragonfly Hour

For the last hour, on the end of this narrow dock,
I've watched the same three dragonflies —
Their double sets of wings intricately laced, iridescent —
Lighting and lifting, lighting again, drifting away, lighting,
Jostled by a heady, refreshing wind.

Like these exquisitely delicate insects, presently resting
(Though they seem about to be blown away, at any second),
I bask in the sun's revitalizing radiance,
Refuse to admit that my existence is fragile, transitory,
Rather glory in this hour of being here, now,

Asking nothing more, nothing less, than to be left to my wiles,
Dedicated to the premeditated pursuit of relaxation,
Between the routine tribulations survival requires,
For the stay fate has allotted us, today.
Husbanding time is what these dragonflies and I do best.

II. Dazzled

As I stare into the far darkness,
There seem to be more stars, in the wide sky,
Than there is room, up there, to accommodate them,
And in wordless wonderment,
I ponder how such a heavenly phenomenon is possible.

Admittedly, being a city dweller,
Accustomed to intrusive light pollution,
Whose white-noise radiance drowns out celestial fulgence,
I never have a chance to witness such incandescence
As illuminates this upper-Wisconsin welkin,

Where the Milky Way and the constellations I memorized,
From my beloved childhood copy of *The Stars for Sam*,
Have been pulled down — a vast field of astral delight
Not even a thousand feet above my eyes.
May these supernumerary stars bury me, in their brilliance!

I. Reason Enough

With each retreat I make, from suburban society,
Returning to Lake Nebagamon gets easier, sweeter.
I'm less and less of a stranger to myself,
More comfortable with whom I'm gradually becoming,
Every time I settle into my shore-nestled cabin,

To witness and listen to the weeks, months, years
Arriving, receding, deciding when the occasion is right,
To resume the blessed unfolding of their majestical seasons,
Oversee the leaves unfurling, from sleep to greening,
The lake flowing, from glistening ripples to groaning ice,

Mid-eighties June and July slipping into chilling September,
Rainbow-hued October blowing into blizzard-frigid December,
Groggy March, restive April, creek-flooded May
Calling me back, for another series of rejuvenating stays,
That I might perpetuate the rendezvous with my future.

This subdued Friday night in mid-August,
Sitting on Lawn Beach Inn's familiar, weathered deck,
Surveying the luminous nine o'clock sky,
I know that just being in the throes of such natural rapture
Is reason enough for my retreats to Lake Nebagamon.

The Stars, the Clouds, and the Lake

XVIII. This Last Afternoon

On this last afternoon of my extended Independence Day stay,
In my cabin beside the shores of this tranquil lake,
I've staked out a modest claim on salvation.

I can't imagine any preoccupation more inspiring,
More spiritually enlightening,
Better for the nurturing of one's flesh and bones and mind,

Than spending unfettered time alone with time,
Listening closely to its rhythms, pacings, syncopations,
The subtle but scrutable wisdoms it makes available

To those of us who recognize it's there/here for the taking, the keeping,
If only we can read the complexities of its ageless palimpsest,
Believe that it really cares about our well-being.

This matchless, eighty-degree last afternoon in Lake Nebagamon,
Time and I have struck a robust covenant
Ensuring that neither of us will ever abandon the other.

XVII. The Things of This World

It's all about getting back to the things of this world,
Things I can see with my pupils, retinas,
Rather than just visualize, symbolize, metaphorize, with my intellect —

Things such as the dragonfly
Alighting on the water bottle I was lifting to my lips,
When some preternatural agency delivered it to me, me to it,

That exquisite creature with two bulging eyes, six hairy legs,
A matched pair of iridescent-lemon, filigreed wings
More intricate than any Art Nouveau brooch or pendant,

And a segmented tail cloisonnéed with green and yellow,
As poised in my presence as I was in its essence,
The two of us assessing each other's quiet majesty . . .

Things such as the mallard overseeing her six ducklings, at feeding,
Not fifty feet from this dock,
From where I watch their tiny heads penetrating the lake, first,

Then, with thrusts and thrashing feet, their bodies plunging under,
Before emerging with fish, plants,
Ceaselessly repeating their ritual, unintimidated by my proximity . . .

Things such as these waters, trees, this cloudy azure sky, the sun . . .
Things at once ordinary and inordinately wondrous . . .
Things that ask nothing of us but our taking the time to notice them

And, in so doing, acknowledge that they, too, possess spirits,
Are also tied to and quickened by the universal soul
That guides all our lives, from nonbeing through eternity.

Just before I say good-twilight to the waves lullabying me,
That dragonfly materializes again, settles atop my bare thigh.
We stare at each other, both of us immortalized.

XVI. The Downhill Side

Around the subdued town,
Gyved to houses and the auditorium's pole,
Which stands at attention,
On the lawn descending to the beach,
Flags droop, in morning's windless fifty degrees.

Nevertheless, their red and white stripes,
Blue fields with half a hundred stars,
Speak an argot of community pride, freedom,
As do the tricolored rainbows
Of semicircular buntings
Yet draped across porch railings, storefronts —
Old Glory spectators of a recent procession,
In whose wake are the thousand or so souls
Scattered around this life-sustaining lake,
Who recognize that the height of their main season
Is already behind them,
On summer's downhill side,
Though three months remain
Before the unmitigable cold takes hold.

For now, this town goes about its doings,
With a sense of fortitude
Befitting a poet penning odes to time's slowness,
All the while knowing he's being seized
In the eaglelike talons and beak of its fleet flight
And that each poem he writes
Is another day leaving these shores.

XV. Spiral Heights

Muted orange, a few hours earlier, this Monday eve,
Now boasting a brilliant alabaster gleam,
The waxing moon scales the sky's orb web

Reaching for its star-stippled zenith,
Above where I sit, on the end of my dock,
And beseeching me to surrender to its enchantments,

Which I do, with the submissiveness of a newborn
Suckling on fantasies, reveries, innocent dreams
Spawned in night's warm womb.

For eons, at least, I watch the lunar orb
As it shimmers in and out of the clouds' silken filaments,
Climbing the brightness of night's spiral heights.

XIV. Rhythms

At ten o'clock, this silent Sunday morning,
While taking a relaxed walk through downtown,
In red shorts, white socks, blue running shoes,
My bare chest absorbing the warmth,
I notice everything's closed, save the Presbyterian church,
Ole's Country Store, Rose's Bakery, Bridge's Tavern.

Two enterprising seagulls are cleaning up the streets,
Feasting on a smorgasbord of July Fourth's leftovers.
I stop at the auditorium door,
To read the posted winners and times of yesterday's race,
Then resume my traipse, going, going.
The village's easy, peaceful rhythms own me.

XIII. The Fifth of July

If last night was a percussive fugue of sounds and sights,
This cabin-quiet Sunday a.m.
Is a melodic hymn to the lake, trees, and sky,
A beatitude in silver, green, and creamy blue.

Gone are the phosphorescent girandoles
That flickered, for hours, like lightning in a violent storm,
Around all ten miles of Lake Nebagamon's shoreline,
After the village's fireworks drifted into afterglow.

Now, the residents of this land are home,
Bathed by a deeply serene sleep and forgetting,
As though no celebrations of freedom ever occurred.
Timelessness has returned to its normal pace.

XII. Phantasmagoria

At 9:00 p.m., the huge, blazing moon,
Hovering, lingering low, on the shadowy horizon,
Begins climbing the trunks of the tall trees
That sway over the deck of this crowded restaurant,
Inching higher, limb by limb, twig by twig, leaf by leaf,
Until, reaching its apex,
It casts its yellow spell across the lake's patina.

I'm captivated, seeing so many boats on the water —
Lambent candles, hundreds of them,
Bobbing gently, like breeze-blown datura blooms —
Their running lights glowing white, red, and green,
Their occupants gathered, in their floating front-row seats,
To take in the immediacy of the explosions
That will weave incandescent tapestries over their heads.

At ten, right on schedule, the fireworks commence —
Rockets, shells screaming hundreds of feet above the beach,
Showering my eyes, with rainbow coruscations,
Shattering the air, with rapid blasts of phantasmagoria
Vying, with the stars, for places in the Milky Way.
I'm in a time, a space, where I've never been,
An unnamed universe palpitating with unmapped constellations.

XI. Happy

This isn't just any old ordinary Saturday;
It's Independence Day, in small-town U.S.A.,
Where, now, at a table outdoors, at Lawn Beach Inn,

I have an overview of the public swimming area, below,
And the sward reaching up from it.
Two hours before the long-awaited fireworks display,

Spectators have appropriated their real estate,
By anchoring folding chairs, spreading blankets, on the grass.
Music drifts my way, from Phoenix Rising, on East Waterfront Drive.

The twilight sky is luminously indigo;
A near-full gauzy moon is visibling itself exquisitely.
Suddenly, a droning pontoon plane lifts off the sedate lake,

Reminding me of the two fighters that did a raucous flyover,
Ten hours earlier,
When the Dragin' Tail Run/Walk had barely concluded,

The colorful, high-octane, wave-pounding speedboats,
Along with the jet skis and pleasure craft,
Hadn't taken to the water, terrifying the wailing loons,

And the parade of vehicles, floats, townsfolk hadn't formed.
As the moon rises, its mesmerizing brightness
Extends, from the far shore, into my twinkling eyes.

Eagerly awaiting the pyrotechnics that will ignite the night,
I realize what this day means to me:
I'm just happy being here . . . being happy, here.

Then come machines far larger than the fire trucks —
Three bright-blue garbage loaders, provided by GT Sanitation
(A homegrown enterprise, source of immense local pride) —
Followed by a late-'60s Corvette, a '70s Cadillac, and a '57 T-Bird,
Followed by two new cars, plastered with political posters
Heralding Assemblyman So-and-So, State Senator Such-and-Such,
Followed by Hanco Utilities' three gleaming modified pickups,

Followed by a brace of dray horses pulling a farm wagon,
Followed by the two grandest entries in the parade:
A Walt Moss Trucking Kenworth tractor and stainless-steel trailer
And the Polaris Racing Team's behemoth rolling garage.
And just when the half-hour humdinger seems spent,
The screeching, flashing, elephantine fire/rescue armada reappears,
Heading up a rerun, to unanimous communal applause.

X. The Best Parade Ever

Where Lake Nebagamon's two main streets meet
And radiate for four blocks north/south, three east/west —
The heart of the heart of downtown,
Which hosts the majority of the village's merchants —
The townspeople and most weekend visitors
(Possibly a thousand, fifteen hundred, or more)
Have congregated, en masse, to watch the annual parade.

To say it'll be a lollapalooza, a bang-up extravaganza,
Would hardly start to do justice
To the giddy patriotic fervor every spectator feels
As the conveyed and pedestrian participants prepare to pass by.
There'll be something for everyone:
A sense of place, name recognition, hurled candy,
The pure, unbridled excitement of just being here, on the Fourth.

At 4:00 p.m. sharp,
The fire trucks, rescue vans, and water tankers
Open the event, with a resounding consequence
(Much like the trunk-to-tail Pachyderm Parade
I remember seeing march off the Ringling Bros. train, in my youth) —
Lemon-yellow, lime-green, carmine, with gold-leaf lettering,
Full light arrays flashing, electronic sirens screeching, wailing.

Though not comparable to equipment used in big-city districts,
These vehicles are prominent reminders
That this lake village and the small towns surrounding it
Are served by volunteer units of civic-minded residents,
Which consider themselves second to none, even the best —
Lake Nebagamon, Highland, Lakeside, Poplar, Brule.
The clapping doesn't stop until they're out of earshot and view.

Next, in quick succession, the procession surges,
Merging a disparate miscellany of incongruous elements:
Four elderly Knights of Columbus, in full-dress regalia;
Floats advertising the Waterfront Bar & Grill, Rose's Bakery,
Young Plumbing & Heating, Dairy Queen/Ole's Country Market,
Chippewa Valley Bank, Kids in Nebagamon;
A cohort of Camp Nebagamon boys wearing craft-project costumes.

IX. Dragin' Tail Run/Walk

The Fourth begins, at the intersection of Waterfront and Lake,
With a palpably exciting fanfare
For the more than six hundred five-mile entrants
(Including sixty teenagers from the boys' camp),
Proudly displaying their bib numbers,
On the fronts of their shirts or shorts,
And the requisite chip timers, around their ankles.

What a splendid morning for a tribute to physical fitness!
The greens are greener, the blues bluer,
Heightened to exultant hues of nature's exuberance.
At once, all goes silent, reverent,
As a volunteer fireman, standing beside the American flag,
Sings the "The Star-Spangled Banner,"
Bravely straining to hit the high notes,

After that, everything shifts from stasis to full throttle.
Walkers, joggers, and serious racers, from counties wide,
Make a most impressive showing,
As the pack disappears into the countryside.
Twice, the extended throng weaves into and out of sight —
Mainly lithe, lean bodies, fighting to best fatigue —
Before reaching the finish, winning a sense of accomplishment.

Soon, all the bananas and cold bottled water,
Distributed outside the auditorium, are gone.
Now, the crowd enters the village's most recent history —
Another Fourth of July celebration begun,
Another race run, not just for the fun of it
But to experience, firsthand, the challenge and struggle
That are the foundations of this nation's prevailing greatness.

VIII. Lake Nebagamon, U.S.A.

Just being seated, this beehive Friday evening,
On Lawn Beach Inn's wraparound deck,
In full view of the water yet alive, at 8:00 p.m.,
With skiers, pontooners, kids swimming at the public beach,
The Stars and Stripes hanging slack, from its flagpole,
On the hill sloping from the red-log auditorium
(This tiny town's cultural lodestone) to the lake,
Distills, in me, feelings of belonging to a dream of becoming,
Coming home to a community I may never leave.

It's infinitely reassuring, knowing I'll be a welcome spectator
At tomorrow's diverse schedule of events:
The "Dragin' Tail Run/Walk," at 9:00 a.m.,
Sponsored by the Lake Nebagamon Volunteer Firefighters;
The 4:00 p.m. parade of floats, walking groups, and vehicles,
Along the town's two main streets;
The Lake Property Association watercraft parade,
Lining up at Honeymoon Point, at 7:00,
And proceeding past the beach and municipal boat landing;

And then the street dance, with music by Phoenix Rising,
Starting at 8:00, running till midnight,
Sponsored by Bridge's Indianhead Tavern and Waterfront Bar & Grill,
During which, at 9:00, Miss Nebagamon will be crowned;
Followed by the *pièce de résistance*, the fireworks display,
Courtesy of the Lions Club and local businesses,
To begin promptly at 10:00, after sun's prolonged setting —
Guaranteed to be even more "ooh"-and-"aah" dazzling
Than all of the past shows combined.

Suddenly, at 9:15, time discovers me,
Finds me entranced, enchanted, beguiled
By the promise of tomorrow's tribute to freedom and democracy.
Having lost myself, in the published roster of events,
I gaze up and see, for the first time,
A tumescent moon rising in the muted-blue sky,
Shining over the soul of Lake Nebagamon,
On the eve of the nation's 234th July Fourth,
And realize that all majestic America is right here, right now.

VII. Complexions

Within a mere three hours, this Friday before the Fourth,
The lake has taken on a complexion I've never seen.
It's mutated from harmonious to frenzied, calm to pulsating.

Speedboats have been arriving in town, all afternoon,
On trailers hitched to tappet-clattering diesel pickup trucks,
Which back them down, into the water, at the public landing,

Set them loose, like giant tillers hoeing up wakes, spray,
Churning the astonished surface, with their propeller blades,
As if this weekend were the extent of their planting season.

Not to be upstaged are myriad thrumming ski boats,
Whining Sea-Doos, and lumbering pontoon boats,
Moving in meaningless circles, straightaways, curlicues.

Meanwhile, each foot of East Waterfront Drive's shoreline,
Every one of its docks but mine, is clotted with people
Come to join Nebagamon's celebration of the nation's birthday —

Relatives, friends, and acquaintances of year-round residents,
Plus a miscellany of tourists, descending on the village,
From Chicago, Minneapolis, Madison, Duluth.

The recession-ravaged country is craving its patriotic fix,
Though skeptical about justifying the excess;
Yet all towns and cities agree that their shows must go on,

And proud Village of Lake Nebagamon is no exception,
Having leaned on its merchants, organizations, individuals,
To raise the $4,500 needed to fund its fireworks display.

By tomorrow noon, the swelling influx of visitors
Should be so colossal as to render this docile community
A metropolis unrecognizable to itself.

As for me, a somewhat frequent sojourner in this refuge,
I've primed myself to join in the revelry,
Knowing that when I return, this August and September,

The lake will have reassumed its subdued complexion
And I'll be able to commune with it, on *my* terms,
Whole again, in the spirit of its ancient embrace.

VI. Keeper of the Realm

It's nine o'clock, on the end of this dock
Jutting a hundred twenty feet out into the lake.
Having slept like an extra-lazy black bear,
Awakening from delicious slumber, I'm groggy, drowsy.
Noise is in happy absence.
Stretching my stiff body, under an unambiguous sun,
Is my most elemental gesture of pleasure.

Out here, I am freedom, in the flesh,
Essence indemnified from death, for life.
I'm a gentle king of all things alive and about to be,
A benign suzerain of drifting ripples and clouds,
Dragonflies and swallows sieving the air, for insects,
A kind ruler of labyrinthine spider webs
Connecting the planks and piers of this dock.

I'm nobody, if not keeper of the realm of cattails and flowers,
Whisker-faced otters, shore-hugging birches and pines,
Waterfowl chaperoning their chicks,
The stars, planets, sun, and moon that regulate day and night.
Quietude is my regal crown, serenity my scepter;
My orb reflects a higher power, to which I owe allegiance:
The inscrutable lord who keeps the universe aligned.

V. Early-Evening Feeding

After yesterday's cold rain had tapered off,
Ominous gray clouds dissipating,
Subliming back into a silvery-white lake and sky,
And night's silence had begun warming slightly,
I stepped out, onto the deck just off the kitchen,
Took the steps to the lower level,
And set about stoking the Weber kettle, with charcoal.

Whenever I spend time here, I revel in this rite,
As though I'm preparing to make sacrifices to the gods,
Propitiations necessarily humbling.
Last evening, my offering was a steelhead trout,
Cooked, carefully, over evenly-low-glowing coals,
And two robust sweet potatoes,
Baking, in aluminum foil, on the edges of the grill.

And during the entire hour it took me to prepare dinner,
I was visited by a quartet of common loons:
Two mates, decorated with green heads, black bills,
Cross-banded backs, white breasts, and red eyes,
Shepherding their pair of brown-hued chicks —
Exquisite wild creatures forming a nuclear family,
Unperturbed by my proximity.

After all, they were preoccupied with feeding,
Too focused on keeping to survival's routine,
To pay me other than cursory heed; I wasn't a predator.
Indeed, they stayed close into shore, in the weed beds,
Both adults continually sliding under the quiverless surface,
To gather fish, crustaceans, plants they'd eat
Or slip into their impatient babies' open mouths.

By the time my food was ready and I'd gone upstairs,
I'd witnessed those nurturing loons
Dutifully complete their foraging,
Seen them glide away, contentedly, into the warm silence,
Those chicks riding high atop their parents' backs.
And I knew that the gods had richly rewarded me,
With one of nature's more glorious gifts.

IV. Aerobatics

This whitish-gray-skied Tuesday a.m.,
The barely rippling, silver-stippled lake before me
Is a vast aerial proving ground
For a squadron of planes practicing intricate maneuvers.
Perhaps they're rehearsing for Saturday's July Fourth celebration.

Their repeated complex, byzantine strafings,
Frenetic twists, erratic lifts and dives,
Rapid reversals of direction,
Resemble those of the fighters I've seen in battle sequences
Captured in historical footage, recreated in WWII movies.

But this is the last day of June 2009;
The location is the peaceful village of Lake Nebagamon;
And the highly skilled, aerobatic flying machines are birds,
Northern rough-winged swallows at early-morning feeding,
Zeroing in on flies, mosquitoes — any airborne insects.

At times, zooming so close to the surface,
They become indistinguishable from their shifting shadows,
Their shadows from chromatic patterns of ever-changing lake.
It's astonishing that they never collide,
Never crash into the water, never cease making their passes.

That I'm fascinated, stimulated, by all this activity,
Comes as no surprise to my eyes, my blood, my psyche.
After all, when time is of negligible consequence
And I'm doing nothing but opening myself to Earth's workings,
Stunning wonders like this disclose themselves,

But only if my senses are capable of seizing, translating,
Illuminating unnoticed mosaics of ineffable grace —
Nature inviting me to unmask the complex, the byzantine,
Divine its ordinary sublimities,
Enter into a dialogue with land, air, and water.

III. Oracle Wind

This northern Wisconsin wind
Is an oracle more primal than any I've ever heard.
For the past three days, it's consulted with my sensibilities,

Sighed distant simplicities, high in the swaying trees,
Deep in the whiplashing pines' needly tufts,
Between the argenteous clusters of fluttering birch leaves,

Stroked the lake's serrated face, with rough love,
Flowed over and under the cantilevered wings
Of bald eagles, gulls, and turkey buzzards.

And I've listened attentively, intuitively,
Knowing that by doing so, with humbleness, faith, and hope,
I just might locate the source of its nuanced wisdom,

Translate the mysteries and secrets it keeps hidden
From all but those curious few who, like me,
Crave being embraced, spoken to, blessed by the wind.

II. Five Sailboats

It's a perfect day for sailors from the boys' camp
To gain hands-on training, learn the foul-weather ropes,
Since Lake Nebagamon is all frothing waves,
A colossal chaos of tumultuous drizzle and squalls
Just below the scudding turbulence of the sky's ubiquitous gray.

From my water's-edge vantage, in this cabin,
I admire the graceful symmetry of five sleek vessels,
As they wrestle the water's choppy surface,
Thread trajectories, tacking back and forth,
And my veins throb, vicariously, with the boys' excitement.

I can still feel the surge of those boats —
Their sails inhaling stupendous blasts of chill air,
Running out from under themselves, as if yanked by Zephyrus —
No matter that fifty-five years separate me
From today's novices manning the helms, tillers, halyards.

Instantly, one of the fleet is caught off guard.
Struck by an oncoming truck of a gust, broadsided,
It hurls its occupants willy-nilly, into the cold chop,
Then turtles, even its jib now invisible;
Only its rudder and hull show above water.

Engrossed, I watch while the three startled teenagers,
Woefully unmatched against the weight of the fiberglass craft,
Hang, helpless, onto the gunwale.
After a half-hour struggle, they bring the sails up,
Right the craft, pull themselves aboard, bail, head back to camp.

Seated here, at the kitchen table, an aged landlubber,
I'm grateful for being safe, warm, dry,
Yet grasp, in my comfort, what I'm missing:
The exhilaration that engenders from taking chances, spills,
The thrill of derring-do that lasts youth a lifetime or two.

I. July Light

It's 9:30, in this northern clime.
The sky's lingering brightness
Hovers above me, its cerulean hue hazed.

Outdoors, at quiet Lawn Beach Inn,
Overlooking the reflective lake,
I see how easy it is to confuse sunset with sunrise.

This breeze-riffled, tree-leafy evening,
I'm as close to immortality as I'll likely be.
Forever and I are almost one,

Where sky and lake and light are interchangeable
And the days, years, eons indistinguishable
From this luminous Friday night.

Independence Days

X. Four Hundred Fifty or So Paces

On this final morning of my five-day stay
In this gorgeous North Woods land of my renascence,
I make one more trek, four hundred fifty or so paces,

From my rented cabin, on the town-side shore of the lake,
Down to the boys' camp, yet living in my past,
To commune with the shadows of my future.

Once inside the back gate,
I'm inundated by the dense scent of freshly greening trees,
Beckoning me into these coverts, to remain forever, if I desire.

But I only have time, today, for an abbreviated circuit,
A brief reading of nature's legendary epic,
To remind myself how tied I am to its beauty and solitude.

Amidst all these empty cabins, paths, spaces,
I listen, intently, for whispers from resident spirits,
Who might be calling me to return to childhood.

Gradually, the silence transforms itself into one voice:
A ubiquitous symphony, on the air,
Being performed, by songbirds, for me alone.

Leaving these woods predisposes my soul to melancholy,
Yet I know why my stay is necessarily evanescent.
Other designs are waiting to shape my destiny,

Among which are two flights I must take, before twilight,
Another pillow upon which to lay my head,
In a city apartment far from cabin and waves.

Now, I've gathered my four hundred fifty or so paces,
Each a steppingstone I've placed in my pockets,
In case sleep beckons my dreams back to Lake Nebagamon.

IX. Early-Morning Swim

An hour has passed
Since I last spoke to the lake.
It's expressing gentle suggestions
Of a rippling effect,
While its quilted stillness,
Having taken on a diffident demeanor,

Is sequestering its secrets
Fifty-six feet below,
In the water's deepest recesses,
Along its ten-odd miles of shoreline,
Within its nine-hundred-plus acres.
The tranquillity speaks to me.

Abruptly, from a distance,
My ears pick up the cries of loons.
Their urgent calls
Heighten the lake's quiescence,
Make its silence all the more inviting.
I dive in.

VIII. Howled

By eight, last evening,
When my appetite had risen to ravenous,
For my having eaten nothing since breakfast's lettuces,

The lake's windy three-day demon-din
Finally exhausted its lashing fury,
Allowing me to safely light a fire in the barbecue pit,

Take my time, in the kitchen, upstairs,
Preparing the asparagus, mushrooms, and garlic cloves
I'd mix into the angel-hair pasta,

While waiting, as the charcoal glowed, slowly,
Into a halo that would sear my thick cut of fresh salmon
To delectable perfection. Dinner was ecstasy's surfeit.

Now, the following dawn, the lake is smooth, peaceful, serene,
Even for this part of Wisconsin.
Nobody would ever guess what malevolence howled.

VII. Naked

Can you recall the last time you sat at a table,
Having breakfast by yourself, naked,
In an isolated cabin, on the shore of a rioting lake,
Feeling so entranced by your sense of release
That nothing else mattered,
Other than that what you were having for breakfast
Was what your body had been craving, for millenniums?

I can and am doing just that, gazing out over a lake
Whose waves are engaged in an atavistic rage,
Hoping to break from their banks, escape into the woods.
I'm satisfying my primal appetite, with baby lettuces —
Red and green romaine, oak leaf, and chard;
Lollo Rossa, red leaf, and Tango;
Mizuna, arugula, mâche, frisée, and radicchio —

Organically grown, succulent lettuces,
To which I've added a healthy helping of cherry tomatoes,
Also raised without pesticide sprays.
Right now, I feel a kindredness, with my surrounds,
So unequivocally pure, so whole, so unadulterated,
That the wind, water, trees, grass, the very food I'm eating,
Are an integral part of me. I am nature.

VI. Minute to Second to Eye Blink

If all I had to rely on,
Were my eyes and ears — mere vision and hearing —
To reckon the texture and tenor of this tumultuous day,
From within my shore-woven cabin,
I'd have to say, without speculation or lesser-informed guessing,
That they surely approximate yesterday's biting chill,
With wind-whipped temperatures in the low fifties, if not below.

But when, having just roused myself from bed,
My veins and bones still filled with sleep,
I tentatively open the kitchen's door and brave the deck,
Facing the furiously thrashed pine trees and shoreline
(The lake's waves are as riled and violent as the trees' limbs),
Expecting to be battered, lashed, by frigid blasts of air,
I'm idling, instead, beside a Florida ocean, in July.

Only, this is northern Wisconsin — Lake Nebagamon — in mid-May,
And it refuses to offer any explanation, at all,
As to its dramatic climactic variations
From day to day, hour to hour, minute to second to eye blink.
Looking out, over the dancing expanse of whitecaps,
Reveling in the eighty-degree wind quivering my flesh,
I'm reminded how viscerally change insists upon itself.

V. The Axeman Village

This crisp, crystalline-blue Tuesday morning,
Not a degree above fifty-two,
I walk, at a brisk clip, from my lakeside retreat,
Down the road, to the sandy back entrance of the boys' camp,
Past its scatter of disassembled docks and gear,
Its landlocked fleet of sailboats, rowboats, canoes,
And enter, all at once, a silent circumambience,
Fitted, so seamlessly, amidst these massive pines,
Within the confines of their sixty-seven shadow-crosshatched acres.

Suddenly, I find myself wandering through the Axeman Village,
Its ramshackle white cabins
Taking notice of the visitor who, once upon a timeless while ago,
Spent two happy months here, twice, when he was twelve and thirteen.
Hands in my pocket, I stand transfixed, mesmerized,
Casting back to summers packed away in memory's trunk and duffel,
Before being awakened, from reverie,
By loon calls rising from the ancient lake,
Reminding me I'm not here by myself

And that, in just about four weeks, these immutable premises
Will fill up with the boisterous, joyous jubilations of youth.
But for now, this hour, these sweet few seconds,
I claim sole ownership
Not of these trees, the cabins, this deep-scented quietude
But of my liberated spirit, my freedom to openly embrace nature,
The peacefulness breathing me alive,
Speaking, to me, a litany of vernal benedictions,
Assuring me that what once was, and is, must unendingly be.

IV. The Gatekeeper

Boisterous and blustery and gusty are what this Monday is.
It's a real corker, a feisty son-of-a-bitch, a devil,
If you happen to be heading into the wind,

Which I am, just this bristling, ear-splitting moment,
Trying to make my way down East Waterfront Drive,
Along the lake, to the rear gate of the shuttered boys' camp,

Where I hope to locate a few ghosts, from my past,
Lurking in the viridescing trees, white clapboard cabins,
And beneath winter's pine-cone-and-brown-needle debris.

My weathering this hike depends, entirely, on the wind,
Whether or not it decides to quit pushing me back, defiantly,
Standing me upright, with its fists to my chest and chin.

Right now, it's treating me as though I were a trespasser.
Perhaps I'd better turn back, wait until this afternoon,
To see if the next gatekeeper recognizes me.

III. Forty-Mile-per-Hour Gusts

A fierce, vociferous wind is agitating the lake,
Whose waves are panicked spectators
Trying to escape a theater an arsonist has set ablaze.

They rush frantically, haphazardly, in a thousand directions,
Some crosswise, others straight into the shore —
A blind, mindless crashing of combers.

Red and white pines guarding this cabin are up in arms —
Their violently wagging boughs, anyway.
Vicious gusts seem intent on tearing limbs from trunks.

I stay indoors, safe yet cowering,
Knowing better than to venture out even onto the deck,
Fearing I might be grabbed up, carried off, aloft,

Into that invisible zone of terrible swirling turbulence,
Cast adrift, blown back to where I left, just yesterday —
Home.

II. Time-Telling

When resettling myself up here, in this northern clime,
For no matter how many ephemeral days,
I find I'm disinclined to strap on my watch.

I prefer having time tell me all that it knows
About water spirits, squalls, migrating clouds,
Pileated woodpeckers boring into trunks of majestic red pines,

Woods dense with decomposing trees, from winter's griefs,
And greening leaves, ferns, and mosses
Heralding the burgeoning new growth of another springtide,

Rather than trying to tell time a thing or two, myself,
About human dimensions and doings cloaked in tricks
My wrist watch just might have up its sleeve.

By now, grown old, at sixty-eight,
While well realizing I'm a mere sapling, in nature's eyes,
What I've come to understand, if anything wise,

Is that existence and its ubiquitous coeval
Are measured not by the beacon-light sweep of a secondhand
But in seasons, cycles, phases, footfalls, and breaths,

Calculated not by numbers on a clock's face
But by instincts, intimations of change on the air,
Shifts of the lake's surface, variations in bird calls, the beats of a heart.

I. Reliquary

The past eight months
Have passed more rapidly than recognition can calculate,
Elapsed, faded, changed into memory vapors
Drifting out of vision, above my aging landscape.
They've taken my senses' lamentations with them.

Now, it's mid-May of a new year,
And my spirit is back here, dwelling, for five days,
In this familiar cabin touching the shore of Lake Nebagamon,
To which, more and more urgently, I return, for succor,
When nothing in my other life satisfies my craving for quiet.

This Sunday morning under the sunny welkin
Is void of sound, save for resonations from a church bell
Beckoning parishioners to worship
And the punctuated calls of two mated-for-life loons
Paddling across the surface of the churning water.

And perhaps it's not silence, at all, I'm trying to find,
So much as time's reliquary, in which to place, for safekeeping,
My soul's holy scrolls —
Poetic reflections on the mysteries of epiphany and ecstasy,
The deepest yearnings of my unaging imagination.

May Gusts and Silences

Prologue
Tonight, I Hear a Loon Wail Twice

Just now, I hear a loon wail twice.
"How can you?" you'd ask, with puzzled demeanor,
Were you sitting with me, on this St. Louis patio,
A twelve-hour drive, at least,
From the lakes of northern Wisconsin and Minnesota,
Where those beautiful, primal creatures summer,
Raise their young, thrive, before migrating south.

And I'd not pause, in shaping my joyous answer:
"Because those haunting wails,
Echoing elegiacally, calling me back,
Are as much a part of my universal being
As my blood's, brain's, and heart's pulsations are.
They're my waking and sleeping dreams,
Oracles prophesying my life's infinite peace."

* *This symbol is used to indicate that a stanza has been divided because of pagination.*

At Dock's End

XIII. Vegetable-Soup Afternoon   *129*
XIV. Measuring Sunrises   *131*
XV. Holiday Travels   *132*
XVI. Two Faces of the Lake   *133*
XVII. Forecast   *134*
XVIII. Snowshoeing, Late Afternoon   *135*
XIX. Other Beauty   *136*
XX. Last Day of the Year   *137*
XXI. Locus   *138*
XXII. Midnight   *139*
XXIII. Off Lorber Point   *140*
XXIV. The End of the Dock   *141*

Epilogue
    A Lake   *143*

    IV. Pontoon Plane   *94*
    V. Monday Sunrise   *95*
    VI. Early-Afternoon Swim   *97*
    VII. Face to Face   *98*
    VIII. My Own Cosmos   *99*
    IX. Amateur Naturalist   *100*
    X. Water and Fire   *101*
    XI. Acorns   *102*
    XII. Southern-Shore Odyssey   *103*
    XIII. Two Geese   *104*
    XIV. Masterpiece   *105*
    XV. Grace   *106*
    XVI. Council Ring   *107*
    XVII. The Stars   *108*
    XVIII. Silver and Gold   *109*
    XIX. Eddie   *110*
    XX. Testament   *111*
    XXI. Real Tears   *112*
    XXII. 6:45   *113*

Christmastide in the Village

    I. Back for Christmas   *117*
    II. Dressing for the Occasion   *118*
    III. The Tree   *119*
    IV. Snowshoeing into Christmas Eve   *120*
    V. December 25   *121*
    VI. Memory   *122*
    VII. The Blizzard   *123*
    VIII. A Change in the White Air   *124*
    IX. Stocking Up   *125*
    X. Snow Spirits   *126*
    XI. Sun   *127*
    XII. Waves   *128*

XVII. The Things of This World   *58*
XVIII. This Last Afternoon   *59*

The Stars, the Clouds, and the Lake

I. Reason Enough   *63*
II. Dazzled   *64*
III. Dragonfly Hour   *65*
IV. Grown-Up Boys   *66*
V. Historical Marker   *67*
VI. Cattails   *69*
VII. Clouds   *70*
VIII. Lives   *71*
IX. Clocking In   *72*
X. Open Windows   *73*
XI. In My Bones   *74*
XII. Each Other's Shadows   *75*
XIII. Blueberry Afternoon   *76*
XIV. Lazy Day   *77*
XV. Aromas   *78*
XVI. Anything Goes   *80*
XVII. The Clouds and the Stars   *81*
XVIII. Family Campers   *82*
XIX. Rap-Rap-Rapping   *83*
XX. Lovers   *84*
XXI. Loons and Crows   *85*
XXII. Eight Nights and Days   *86*
XXIII. Morning Mist   *87*

Sunrises and Sunsets

I. This Moment   *91*
II. Whispering   *92*
III. Quiet Saturday in Lake Nebagamon   *93*

Contents

Prologue
Tonight, I Hear a Loon Wail Twice 25

May Gusts and Silences
I. Reliquary 29
II. Time-Telling 30
III. Forty-Mile-per-Hour Gusts 31
IV. The Gatekeeper 32
V. The Axeman Village 33
VI. Minute to Second to Eye Blink 34
VII. Naked 35
VIII. Howled 36
IX. Early-Morning Swim 37
X. Four Hundred Fifty or So Paces 38

Independence Days
I. July Light 41
II. Five Sailboats 42
III. Oracle Wind 43
IV. Aerobatics 44
V. Early-Evening Feeding 45
VI. Keeper of the Realm 46
VII. Complexions 47
VIII. Lake Nebagamon, U.S.A. 48
IX. Dragin' Tail Run/Walk 49
X. The Best Parade Ever 50
XI. Happy 52
XII. Phantasmagoria 53
XIII. The Fifth of July 54
XIV. Rhythms 55
XV. Spiral Heights 56
XVI. The Downhill Side 57

*I will arise and go now, and go to Innisfree,
And a small cabin build there, of clay and wattles made:
Nine bean-rows will I have there, a hive for the honey bee,
And live alone in the bee-loud glade.*

*And I shall have some peace there, for peace comes dropping slow,
Dropping from the veils of the morning to where the cricket sings;
There midnight's all a glimmer, and noon a purple glow,
And evening full of the linnet's wings.*

*I will arise and go now, for always night and day
I hear lake water lapping with low sounds by the shore;
While I stand on the roadway, or on the pavements grey,
I hear it in the deep heart's core.*
— William Butler Yeats, "The Lake Isle of Innisfree"

I have discovered that I am not alone in my listening; that almost everyone is listening for something, that the search for places where the singing may be heard goes on everywhere. It seems to be part of the hunger that all of us have for a time when we were closer to lakes and rivers, to mountains and meadows and forests, than we are today.
— Sigurd F. Olson, *The Singing Wilderness*

For my beloved son, Troika.

May you and I

"Keep the fires burning!"

Acknowledgments

Once again, it has been my immense privilege to share my passion for poetry with my Time Being Books editors of two decades, Sheri Vandermolen and Jerry Call, and to have them reciprocate my elation, by giving me every degree of their editorial expertise. Without their eager and unstinting desire to help bring these poems to their most expressive measure, I would have fallen disappointingly short of my artistic and aesthetic conception for this book.

Trilogy Maya Mattson, also of Time Being Books, has enhanced these poems, with insightful suggestions that made me reevaluate certain critical elements of this work.

I'm grateful to the following publications, in which these poems appeared, in earlier versions: *Acumen* ("Other Beauty"); *Avocet* ("Silver and Gold" and "Snowshoeing into Christmas Eve"); *Convergence* ("Open Windows"); *Illuminations* ("Time-Telling"); *Main Street Rag* ("My Own Cosmos"); *Poem* ("Keeper of the Realm"); and *The Storyteller* ("Open Windows").

Copyright © 2011 by Louis Daniel Brodsky

All rights reserved under International and Pan-American Copyright Conventions. No part of this book shall be reproduced in any form (except by reviewers for the public press) without written permission from the publisher:

> Time Being Books®
> 10411 Clayton Road
> St. Louis, Missouri 63131

Time Being Books® is an imprint of Time Being Press®, St. Louis, Missouri.

Time Being Press® is a 501(c)(3) not-for-profit corporation.

Time Being Books® volumes are printed on acid-free paper.

ISBN 978-1-56809-140-2 (paperback)

Library of Congress Cataloging-in-Publication Data for the first title in this series:

Brodsky, Louis Daniel.
 At water's edge : poems of Lake Nebagamon / by Louis Daniel Brodsky. — 1st ed.
 v. cm.
 ISBN: 978-1-56809-126-6 (v. 1 : pbk. : alk. paper) 1. Nature--Poetry. 2. Lake Nebagamon (Wis. : Village)--Poetry. 3. Wisconsin--Poetry. I. Title. II. Title: Poems of Lake Nebagamon. III. Title: Lake Nebagamon.
 PS3552.R623A93 2010
 811'.54—dc22

2010011682

Cover design by Jeff Hirsch
Cover photograph courtesy of the author
Book design and typesetting by Trilogy M. Mattson

Manufactured in the United States of America
First Edition, first printing (2011)

At Dock's End

Poems of Lake Nebagamon, Volume Two

Louis Daniel Brodsky

Time Being Books
An imprint of Time Being Press
St. Louis, Missouri

Bibliography *(coedited with Robert Hamblin) (continued)*

Faulkner: A Comprehensive Guide to the Brodsky Collection: Volume I, The Biobibliography   (1982)

Faulkner: A Comprehensive Guide to the Brodsky Collection: Volume II, The Letters   (1984)

Faulkner: A Comprehensive Guide to the Brodsky Collection: Volume III, *The De Gaulle Story*   (1984)

Faulkner: A Comprehensive Guide to the Brodsky Collection: Volume IV, *Battle Cry*   (1985)

Country Lawyer and Other Stories for the Screen by William Faulkner   (1987)

Faulkner: A Comprehensive Guide to the Brodsky Collection: Volume V, Manuscripts and Documents   (1989)

Stallion Road: A Screenplay by William Faulkner   (1989)

Biography

William Faulkner, Life Glimpses   (1990)

Fiction

Between Grief and Nothing *(novel)*   (1964)*

Between the Heron and the Wren *(novel)*   (1965)*

"Dink Phlager's Alligator" and Other Stories   (1966)*

The Drift of Things *(novel)*   (1966)*

Vineyard's Toys *(novel)*   (1967)*

The Bindle Stiffs *(novel)*   (1968)*

Yellow Bricks *(short fictions)*   (1999)

Catchin' the Drift o' the Draft *(short fictions)*   (1999)

This Here's a Merica *(short fictions)*   (1999)

Leaky Tubs *(short fictions)*   (2001)

Rated Xmas *(short fictions)*   (2003)

Nuts to You! *(short fictions)*   (2004)

Pigskinizations *(short fictions)*   (2005)

With One Foot in the Butterfly Farm *(short fictions)*   (2009)

Getting to Unknow the Neighbors *(short fictions)*   (2010)

Memoir

The Adventures of the Night Riders, Better Known as the Terrible Trio *(with Richard Milsten)*   (1961)*

* *Unpublished*

The Eleventh Lost Tribe: Poems of the Holocaust   (1998)*
Toward the Torah, Soaring: Poems of the Renascence of Faith   (1998)
Voice Within the Void: Poems of *Homo supinus*   (2000)
The Swastika Clock: Endlösung Poems   (2000)*
Rabbi Auschwitz: Poems of the Shoah   (2000)* (2009)
Shadow War: A Poetic Chronicle of September 11 and Beyond, Volume One   (2001) (2004)
The Complete Poems of Louis Daniel Brodsky: Volume Two, 1967–1976
   (edited by Sheri L. Vandermolen)   (2002)
Shadow War: A Poetic Chronicle of September 11 and Beyond, Volume Two   (2002) (2004)
Shadow War: A Poetic Chronicle of September 11 and Beyond, Volume Three   (2002) (2004)
Shadow War: A Poetic Chronicle of September 11 and Beyond, Volume Four   (2002) (2004)
Shadow War: A Poetic Chronicle of September 11 and Beyond, Volume Five   (2002) (2004)
Regime Change: Poems of America's Showdown with Iraq, Volume One   (2002)*
Heavenward   (2003)*
Regime Change: Poems of America's Showdown with Iraq, Volume Two   (2003)*
Regime Change: Poems of America's Showdown with Iraq, Volume Three   (2003)*
The Location of the Unknown: Shoah Poems   (2004)*
The Complete Poems of Louis Daniel Brodsky: Volume Three, 1976–1980
   (edited by Sheri L. Vandermolen)   (2004)
Peddler on the Road: Days in the Life of Willy Sypher   (2005)
Combing Florida's Shores: Poems of Two Lifetimes   (2006)
Showdown with a Cactus: Poems Chronicling the Prickly Struggle Between the Forces
   of Dubya-ness and Enlightenment, 2003–2006   (2006)
A Transcendental Almanac: Poems of Nature   (2006)
Once upon a Small-Town Time: Poems of America's Heartland   (2007)
Still Wandering in the Wilderness: Poems of the Jewish Diaspora   (2007)
The World Waiting to Be: Poems About the Creative Process   (2008)
The Complete Poems of Louis Daniel Brodsky: Volume Four, 1981–1985
   (edited by Sheri L. Vandermolen)   (2008)
Unser Kampf: Poems of the Final Solution   (2008)*
Dine-Rite: Breakfast Poems   (2008)
Rien Sans Amour: Love Poems for Jane   (2009)*
By Leaps and Bounds: Volume Two of *The Seasons of Youth*   (2009)
At Water's Edge: Poems of Lake Nebagamon, Volume One   (2010)
Seizing the Sun and Moon: Volume Three of *The Seasons of Youth*   (2010)
In the Liberation Camps: Poems of the Endlösung   (2011)*
At Dock's End: Poems of Lake Nebagamon, Volume Two   (2011)

Bibliography **(coedited with Robert Hamblin)**
Selections from the William Faulkner Collection of Louis Daniel Brodsky: A Descriptive
   Catalogue   (1979)

Books by Louis Daniel Brodsky

Poetry

Five Facets of Myself   (1967)* (1995)
The Easy Philosopher   (1967)* (1995)
"A Hard Coming of It" and Other Poems   (1967)* (1995)
The Foul Rag-and-Bone Shop   (1967)* (1969, exp.)* (1995, exp.)
Points in Time   (1971)* (1995) (1996)
Taking the Back Road Home   (1972)* (1997) (2000)
Trip to Tipton and Other Compulsions   (1973)* (1997)
"The Talking Machine" and Other Poems   (1974)* (1997)
Tiffany Shade   (1974)* (1997)
Trilogy: A Birth Cycle   (1974) (1998)
Cold Companionable Streams   (1975)* (1999)
Monday's Child   (1975) (1998)
Preparing for Incarnations   (1975)* (1976, exp.) (1999) (1999, exp.)
The Kingdom of Gewgaw   (1976) (2000)
Point of Americas II   (1976) (1998)
La Preciosa   (1977) (2001)
Stranded in the Land of Transients   (1978) (2000)
The Uncelebrated Ceremony of Pants-Factory Fatso   (1978) (2001)
Birds in Passage   (1980) (2001)
Résumé of a Scrapegoat   (1980) (2001)
Mississippi Vistas: Volume One of *A Mississippi Trilogy*   (1983) (1990)
You Can't Go Back, Exactly   (1988, two eds.) (1989) (2003, exp.)
The Thorough Earth   (1989)
Four and Twenty Blackbirds Soaring   (1989)
Falling from Heaven: Holocaust Poems of a Jew and a Gentile *(with William Heyen)*   (1991)
Forever, for Now: Poems for a Later Love   (1991)
Paper-Whites for Lady Jane: Poems of a Midlife Love Affair   (1992) (1995)
Mistress Mississippi: Volume Three of *A Mississippi Trilogy*   (1992)
A Gleam in the Eye: Volume One of *The Seasons of Youth*   (1992) (2009)
Gestapo Crows: Holocaust Poems   (1992)
The Third Year's a Charm: Later-Love Poems   (1993)*
The Capital Café: Poems of Redneck, U.S.A.   (1993)
Disappearing in Mississippi Latitudes: Volume Two of *A Mississippi Trilogy*   (1994)
Variations on a Love Theme: Poems for Janie   (1995)*
A Mississippi Trilogy: A Poetic Saga of the South   (1995)*
The Complete Poems of Louis Daniel Brodsky: Volume One, 1963–1967
   (edited by Sheri L. Vandermolen)   (1996)
Three Early Books of Poems by Louis Daniel Brodsky, 1967–1969: *The Easy Philosopher*,
   "A Hard Coming of It" and Other Poems, and *The Foul Rag-and-Bone Shop*
   (edited by Sheri L. Vandermolen)   (1997)

At Dock's End

this case, Lake Nebagamon), the healing grace and tranquillity of nature. "Everyone should have a lake in the valley of his soul," Brodsky teaches us, and for those of us not fortunate enough to have experienced such a sojourn, these poems make such a lake come alive. Through reading this book, each one of us can immerse himself both in Lake Nebagamon and in the lake of the imagination and be assured that "what once was, and is, must unendingly be." This book of poems is highly recommended.
— Yakov Azriel, author of *Threads from a Coat of Many Colors: Poems on Genesis* and *In the Shadow of a Burning Bush: Poems on Exodus*

Louis Daniel Brodsky's poetry is an antidote to our plugged-in society. Once exposed, as a child, to the beauty and solitude of the North Woods, Brodsky was a goner. He's returned often, as an adult, spending weeks, in solitude, in a cabin at the shore of his beloved lake — and his poems shine with the glory of it all.
— Nardie and Sally Stein, former directors of Camp Nebagamon for Boys

At the end of the first decade of the twenty-first century, when technology and postmodern crises loom large, Louis Daniel Brodsky pauses to listen to silences, to look at horizons, and to speak to senses. In clear and comforting sounds, he forces us to remember not tranquillity but the multitudes of life, the vicissitudes that assault us and from which poetry, as a practice of space, rescues us. This is nature poetry for our age and a seer's clairvoyant vision, from Lake Nebagamon, which, in calming our everyday lives, amidst this century's tumultuous fractures, reminds us of Walden Pond and Thoreau's best contemplations.
— Thadious M. Davis, author of *Games of Property: Law, Race, Gender, and Faulkner's **Go Down, Moses*** and *Nella Larsen, Novelist of the Harlem Renaissance: A Woman's Life Unveiled*

This exquisite blizzard began at midnight.
Now, another six to eight fluffy inches of powder,
Accumulated on top of the nine or so fallen a week ago, . . .

It *is* exquisite. Or take this line, from "Snow Spirits":

The iced-over, snow-covered lake is faceted with fire, . . .

The beauty is almost palpable.
To read Louis Daniel Brodsky's poetry is to unlock an interior meditation within us all . . . if only we can listen for it.
— Charles Rammelkamp, author of *Castleman in the Academy*, *The Book of Life*, *The Secret Keepers*, and *Go to Hell*

Like Wordsworth, Whitman, and Frost, Brodsky evolves complex meditations on the relation of individual mind to nature, memory, and its own perceptions. Yet he is always himself. As he writes, in one of the most striking poems, "It's all about getting back to the things of this world." Brodsky delivers that, and more.
— George Bornstein, Professor Emeritus of English, University of Michigan, and author of many scholarly books, including *The Colors of Zion: Blacks, Jews, and Irish from 1845 to 1945*

Louis Brodsky has tapped into the heartwood of the North Country and shares, with us, the treasure he has found. He is a lucky man. He has a place in the woods up north. Now, thanks to the gift of his verse, the rest of us do, too.
— Sam Cook, outdoors writer, *Duluth News Tribune*, and author of *Up North*, *Friendship Fires*, *Quiet Magic*, and *Camp Sights*

Louis Daniel Brodsky's new collection of poems, *At Dock's End: Poems of Lake Nebagamon, Volume Two*, is a poetic journal of one man's sojournings in the woodlands of Lake Nebagamon, in northern Wisconsin. Brodsky shows us, amidst the stress and noise of modern urban society, that man needs to return to the solitude of nature, in order to restore his soul. Like Thoreau at Walden Pond and Wordsworth in northwestern England's Lake District, Brodsky finds, in the beauty of a lake and its surroundings (in

Praise for
At Dock's End: Poems of Lake Nebagamon

While Louis Daniel Brodsky is nowhere near the end of his creativity, it is true that with the publication of *At Dock's End*, he will be reaching his three-score and ten, and he has certainly achieved a kind of wisdom that is evident throughout this collection. Indeed, as he writes, in "Time Telling," the second poem of the collection:

> By now, grown old, at sixty-eight,
> While well realizing I'm a mere sapling, in nature's eyes,
> What I've come to understand, if anything wise,
>
> Is that existence and its ubiquitous coeval
> Are measured not by the beacon-light sweep of a secondhand
> But in seasons, cycles, phases, footfalls, and breaths, . . .

Brodsky has been called a modern Thoreau, a twenty-first-century Whitman, and these poems bear that claim out, in their description of and reverence for the natural world and a man's place in it. *At Dock's End* continues the contemplation of Lake Nebagamon, in Wisconsin, begun in *At Water's Edge* — and, even before that, in *You Can't Go Back, Exactly* — and how the generations overlap in a cyclical fashion, within the context of the vast timelessness of nature. Brodsky captures this timelessness in his descriptions of the woods, the lake, the storms, yet against this background, he shows us the poignance of the comparatively brief life of a man, and therein lies the wisdom of the work.

Whereas the poems in *At Water's Edge* take place in autumn, *At Dock's End* begins in the spring and plunges headlong, through the year, past the summer residents and celebrations that flare and fade, returning to the cozy, contemplative melancholy isolation of fall and the stark reality of the cold, snow-heavy winter, at the end of the year, when all lies dormant. But just as Shelley wrote, in "Ode to the West Wind," "If winter comes, can spring be far behind?" so Brodsky points, at the end of the collection, to yet another season in the endless natural cycle of the woods and the lake, and to another volume of poetry in this remarkable series:

> At this rate, by late April, when the ice should be melted,
> Or at least as mid-May green awakens around the lake,
>
> I'll be able to walk out on my dock again . . .

Yet the winter is also beautiful. Indeed, in his descriptions of color and scene across the half-year span this collection embraces, Brodsky brings alive the overwhelming beauty of the woods and the lake, in poems like "Early-Morning Swim," "July Light," "Spiral Heights," "The Things of This World," and dozens of others — the entire third and fourth sections ("The Stars, the Clouds, and the Lake"; "Sunrises and Sunsets"). "Snowshoeing into Christmas Eve," from the final section, begins: